D1564142

The Investor's Guide to
Penny Mining Stocks

The Investor's Guide to Penny Mining Stocks

Robert Bishop

KCI Communications, Inc.
Alexandria, Va.

All inquiries concerning this book should be directed to KCI
Communications, Inc., 1101 King St., Suite 400, Alexandria, VA
22314.

Library of Congress Cataloging-in-Publication Data

Bishop, Robert, 1949-
    The investor's guide to penny mining stocks.

       1. Stocks. 2. Gold. 3. Silver. 4. Speculation.
I. Title. II. Title: Penny mining stocks.
HG6041.B49 1986   332.6'722   86-20038
ISBN 0-937583-01-4

Table of Contents

Acknowledgments

Much of the information in this book is the product of research on behalf of my monthly newsletter, *Penny Mining Stock Report*. Most of what I have learned in the five years since I made my first penny stock purchase is the result of help I've been given along the way and some of those who've helped deserve special mention.

Howard Ruff, for whom I once worked and wrote my first words on penny stocks, gave me the opportunity to work my way out of a job and into a newsletter. For that I will be forever grateful. Howard also had the good sense to insist that I team up with someone who knew his way around the penny markets. That person was Jerry Pogue, undoubtedly the best known and highest volume penny mining broker in North America.

Jerry introduced me around Vancouver, shared his valuable contacts and insight and was more responsible than anyone else for my getting up on the learning curve in this field. Jerry also sold me my first penny stock, Bull Run at $.59, which I had occasion to sell some three months and 900 percent later (three others I selected at random went nowhere). Any thoughts I had that penny stocks could be picked at random were quickly dispelled by my exposure to Jerry's fundamental approach.

Several other people have been of significant help to me, both as sources of information for this book and as contacts I value on an ongoing basis. This group includes, but is certainly not limited to, Norm Burmeister, Doug Casey, George Cross, Mike Doherty, Gerry Fabbro, Peter Ferderber, Bill Green, Norman Lamb, Phil Lindstrom, John Lydall, Ian McAvity, Dan Rosenthal and John Woods. I greatly value my association with these people and many others too numerous to mention. While freely acknowledging their contributions and valued advice, I alone am responsible for any errors and omissions in the following pages. In all cases, the opinions are mine alone.

My assistant, Brent Vogel, functions as the right side of my brain; his help on computer-related matters and all other aspects of production has been invaluable to me. I'm also grateful to the people at KCI Communications for their help, especially for the editorial assistance of Christina Gibson and Roger Conrad.

My wife, Nancy, and sons, Justin and Timothy, deserve a special thanks for their understanding of my sometimes ir-regular hours and the routine sacrifices they make during my deadlines and frequent travel. Lastly, I'd like to thank my subscribers, the people who allow me to make a living in the fascinating and highly profitable world of gold stocks.

Preface

This book is a compilation of articles, many of which have previously appeared in *Penny Mining Stock Report*, my monthly newsletter specializing in low-priced precious metals mining stocks. While some of the advice that applies to penny mining stocks is also applicable to investment-grade mining stocks, this book is not the answer to all of your questions about gold stocks. Instead, it concentrates on the more speculative end of the market, ideally where greater risks are accompanied by the prospect of greater rewards.

While this book was written in August 1987, it did not go to press until after the stock market plunged on October 19, 1987. Because of the current volatility of the markets, please keep in mind that some circumstances might change dramatically by the time you read this.

The purpose of this book is not to convince its readers that gold has a bright future in the next few years, but rather to define some of the ways to profit from that occurrence. I happen to believe that gold's prospects for price appreciation are excellent, and those who partake of the advice within this book should share in that belief. I expect gold to be one of the main beneficiaries of government's ineptitude with money and that carefully selected gold stocks will greatly outperform the metal itself.

Many others have written about the larger economic questions that will ultimately govern gold's course in the years ahead, and I won't attempt to repeat or distill their efforts. What I will do early in the book is outline some of the reasons I am optimistic about gold's future and, more important, convey some information that I believe will aid you in leveraging your investments in low-priced precious metals stocks.

This book is about an inherently speculative subject, and while experience and information can reduce some of these risks, there is no escaping the high-risk nature of owning shares in the low-priced mining and resource exploration stocks commonly known as "penny" stocks. Lest there be any confusion about the speculative nature of the market in these stocks, I would advise that money you're not prepared to lose should not be invested in this sector of the market. With that ultimate in caveats behind us, let me also add that I think penny mining shares will be the most profitable way to invest in gold during the bull market that is now developing.

Despite the risks just cited, I said earlier that this book is *not* about gambling. What this book is about *is* reducing some of the inherent risks of this little-understood marketplace—and maximizing the rewards that accrue to investors with knowledge and foresight to own these shares before the risks are reduced and the greatest rewards are history. As for the future, may yours be filled with profits.

Robert Bishop
Lafayette, California

1

"It's impossible to avoid a precipice when one follows a road that leads nowhere else."

J.B. Say, *Treatise on Political Economy*, 1880

Why Penny Mining Stocks?

This book is about getting money to the other side of that precipice. How much money investors devote to that pursuit is a highly individual matter, one that will be based largely on one's own economic philosophy. My own philosophy, a belief that underlies all that is advocated in these pages, is that gold has a strong future over the next few years. How strong a future and how many years are unknown to me, but gold has been in a rising market since February 1985 and, for the time being, my inclination is to bet on a continuation of this trend.

The established uptrend of gold prices will reverse itself in time—and there will be setbacks even during its upward climb—but as long as our society chooses to defer what cannot be paid for today, gold has a much stronger future than any of the transient currencies on the scene today. In the past, borrowed money has always equaled borrowed time and there's little now that leads me to conclude that this time will be any different. Traditionally, gold prices have been the beneficiary of fiscal excess; these excesses are among the reasons gold is selling for approximately $450 as this is written and why I believe it will move much higher before the end of the current economic cycle.

This is not a book detailing the reasons I believe gold is headed higher in the years ahead, but rather a framework of information and specific stock recommendations designed to help investors profit from that occurrence. Still, to understand why I think gold has a strong future—and gold stocks stronger still—requires a brief review of where gold prices have been, some of the reasons behind its gyrations and some speculation on the prospects for future profits in gold.

It's easy to lose sight of today, but it was not so many years ago that gold's price was fixed at $35 per ounce. In 1971, however, gold was severed from the dollar and freed to seek its own level in the marketplace. Just three years later, the price of gold had risen to more than $160 per ounce. Talk of gold sales from the stockpiles of the International Monetary Fund and the U.S. Treasury, coupled with a recession, sent gold's price down to $102.50 in August 1976. (Incidentally, the obituaries on gold from that period are indistinguishable from those heard in June 1982 and February 1985 and predictions of gold's imminent demise being heard in some quarters today.) In the three years following the August 1976 low, gold more than tripled in price; by January 1980, gold had posted a high of $850 an ounce. Platinum peaked at $1,050 and silver at $50 per ounce.

To many, current gold prices may appear depressed, especially to those who bought gold at $600 several years ago. Even those who didn't have the misfortune to buy at much higher prices than those prevailing today remember that gold was $850 in 1980. In 1982, and again in 1985, gold traded for less than $300; even the current price of about $450 is substantially less than the record price attained in January 1980. As for the people who bought gold during this period and held it in expectation of profit, it's not difficult to understand their preoccupation with $850 gold. Their perception of the gold market, indeed the perception of many who didn't "buy the top," is that gold has been a loser for almost a decade. This not-uncommon view of gold is that it's a commodity selling for little more than half what it did at its peak.

The North American Gold Boom

From my perspective, the bull market in gold has not even begun to get under way. But there's a new and even more exciting development: the boom that's going on right now in North American gold mining.

In the past 400 years alone, the major centers of gold mining in the free world have shifted from Latin America to Australia to South Africa, which alone mined about half of the non-Communist world's production in 1986. In contrast, the United States and Canada together mined only 16.9 percent. But let's look at the trend. While South African gold production actually declined 5 percent from 1980 through 1986, North American production was up 163 percent.

World Gold Supply 1980-1986
(in tonnes)

	1980	1981	1982	1983	1984	1985	1986
South Africa	675	658	664	680	683	673	640
Canada	52	53	67	73	86	90	108
USA	30	44	45	63	66	79	108
Australia	17	18	27	31	39	59	75

	1980	1981	1982	1983	1984	1985	1986
Brazil	35	35	35	59	62	72	67
Philippines	22	25	31	33	34	37	40
Papua/							
New Guinea	14	17	18	18	19	32	36
Other							
Free World	114	131	141	158	171	191	207
Total Non-							
Communist	959	981	1028	1,115	1,160	1,233	1,281
Soviet Sales	90	280	203	93	205	210	402
Net Offic. Sales	-	-	-	142	85	-	-
Scrap	482	232	237	289	284	299	465
Net Inv. Sales	-	269	163	-	62	169	-
Total	1,531	1,762	1,631	1,639	1,796	1,911	2,148

Source: Consolidated Gold Fields, *Gold 1987.*

While gold production in South Africa has peaked, new discoveries are being made, mines developed and gold bars poured all over North America. Here are eight of the largest producing gold mines in North America in 1986, with their production costs.

North American Mines
1986 Production

Mine	Ounces	Cost/Oz.
Golden Giant	255,000	C$153
Page-Williams	233,000	C$223
Doyon, Quebec	213,000	C$233
Homestake, S.D.	342,000	US$298
Jerritt Canyon	270,000	C$174
Campbell, Ontario	229,000	C$148
Fortitude, Nev.	259,000	US$147
Newmont (Carlin)	474,000	US$172

Source: *Mining Journal Gold Service International Quarterly.*

Can the gold mining industry in North America compete internationally over the long term? The main competitor now is, of course, South Africa. But notice the rising production costs per ounce for the major South African mining companies listed in the table below. From July 1985 to July 1986, costs were well below those of the larger North American mines. The next year, costs evened up a bit.

Production Costs
South African Mines

	7/85-7/86	7/86-7/87
Blyvooruitzicht	$187.77	$250.51
Buffelsfontein	169.35	255.84
Cons. Modder	129.70	224.18
Deelkraal	199.75	219.60
Driefontein	107.89	131.50
Elandsrand	162.98	231.34
E.T. Cons.	168.79	172.86
Hartebeest	130.61	155.28
Kinross	131.15	200.00
Kloof	99.33	116.61
Randfontein	141.16	215.67
Southvaal	123.17	187.73
Unisel	113.20	177.20
Vaal Reefs	162.75	219.22
Winklehaak	133.21	188.65
Western Deep	149.51	209.19

Source: *Mining Journal Gold Service International Quarterly.*

While the two mining industries can coexist, several things are happening now that could help North America someday replace South Africa as the world's leading gold mining center.

Unlike the North American mining industry, South African mining is dependent on the availability of a large, cheap, unskilled migrant work force from neighboring states

and from the quasi-independent "homelands." This is because South African mines are sometimes two to three miles
underground and require cheap labor on a large scale to extract the gold. The major discoveries in South Africa were
made 50 years ago, so mines must go increasingly deeper to
get less gold. Sooner or later they will come up against the
law of diminishing returns and the center of world gold
mining will shift elsewhere, assuming revolution doesn't
send it elsewhere much sooner. Meanwhile, production
costs should continue to rise.

Where does this leave the North American mining industry? The eventual demise of South African mining may
be months or decades away. But North American discoveries are already challenging the enormity of South Africa's
reserves.

Two of the most prolific finds of the 1980s were in the
Hemlo region of Ontario and the Carlin trend in Nevada. The
Hemlo is being developed on a large scale by myriad
companies in a variety of locations. The Page-Williams and
Golden Giant mines are two of the area's largest. Page-
Williams alone is expected to produce 500,000 ounces of
gold per year by 1991, making it the largest mining opera-
tion to date in North America.

But more recent discoveries in the Carlin trend may rival
even that mine. Already, Newmont Mining's operations in
the region are producing nearly 500,000 ounces of gold annually. Drill results from properties owned by American
Barrick Resources and Franco Nevada Resources may prove
to be equally lucrative. The 25-mile-long Carlin belt has
produced more than 14 million ounces since 1964 and has
another 20 million ounces of proven reserves.

Other promising discoveries have been made in several
areas of North America, including the LaRonge belt of
Saskatchewan and others in Colorado and South Carolina.

The bottom line is that North American gold mining is a

growth industry that will reap profits for investors who get into its companies on the ground floor. As North American mining begins to blossom and South African mining fades, the major producers will enrich their shareholders. But the best profit opportunities will be in the junior issues, the so-called penny mining shares.

Small Is Better

What do we mean by "penny mining shares"? True penny mining share prices move up or down dramatically with relatively small amounts of buying and selling. Generally, these are stocks trading for under $10. But the most important factor distinguishing them is the size of their market—their market capitalization.

Market capitalization is determined by multiplying the number of outstanding shares a company has by its share price. For example, a company trading for $2 a share with 1 million shares outstanding has a market capitalization of $2 million.

Market capitalization gives you an idea of how the market values a company—whether it is cheap or dear at current prices. At $10 per share, a company with 1 million shares out has a market capitalization of $10 million. At $1 a share, a company with 100 million shares outstanding has a market capitalization of $100 million. Thus, paradoxically, the $1 stock is actually more expensive than the $10 stock.

Why is this important? Simply put, if $5 million is invested in a company with a $10 million market capitalization, the effect will be much more dramatic than if it were invested in a $100 million company. The lower the market capitalization, the greater the share price volatility, hence the upside potential.

Penny Stock Comparison
1978 Low to 1980 High

Stock	'78 Low	'80 High	Yield/$1K
Belmoral	$ .85	$40.25	$ 47,353
Carolin	1.85	57.00	30,811
Cons. Cinola	.54	22.00	40,741
Gold Reserve	.50	4.50	9,000
Gold Standard	.08	4.25	53,125
Lincoln	.59	20.00	33,898
Little Squaw	.19	3.00	15,789
Pegasus	.68	16.25	23,897
Silver Stack	1.01	36.50	36,139
Sudbury	.19	5.50	28,947
Tournigan	.55	4.50	8,182
T.R.V. Minerals	.85	39.50	46,471

Source: National Securities Corp.

In the broad stock market, small capitalization stocks or growth stocks have traditionally outperformed the large capitalization blue chips over the long haul. This is primarily because the growth companies are by nature getting larger. But it is also a function of mathematics. For example, if a $1 stock goes up $1 to become a $2 stock, you have a 100 percent profit. By contrast, a $100 stock must rise $100 to give you the same 100 percent gain.

The history of penny mining stock markets shows the greater potential of small capitalization stocks. For example, the average stock on the Spokane exchange rose 15,700 percent from 1960 to 1968. The table above shows some of the more dramatic examples of the 1980 gold boom's effect on small stocks. A lot of money chasing a few shares is quite awe inspiring.

Choosing Shares

Of course, choosing the right penny mining stocks to buy can be a problem. Whereas investing in a company like Newmont basically only requires you to make a decision about which way gold is going, buying a penny share makes you think about the company's management, finances, promoters, current ownership, market capitalization and type of property held.

Further, there is a wide credibility gap in the penny mining industry. Someone once said that a mine is a hole in the ground with a liar at the entrance. Herein lies the main disadvantage of buying penny mining stocks: lack of reliable and readily available information on the companies. Aside from all the problems associated with opening a mine (99 percent of all wildcat explorations amount to no more than an exchange listing), a dishonest promoter can lure you into a sucker situation if you throw caution to the wind.

So how do you pick penny stocks? It's absolutely true that when the wind blows even the turkeys will fly. When the kind of boom comes along that I'm expecting, all (or almost all) of the stocks should take off as the public moves in droves into the mines. This is what happened in 1980 and it could easily happen again.

If you want to play this kind of broad move, a purely random approach to stock picking should do nicely. A random portfolio will yield more than a few dogs, but it should keep you from buying only the highly touted, high-priced pennies that everyone has heard about. But if you're willing to research companies on your own, you can avoid the dogs. Picking stocks is more difficult than picking trends, however. The strategy of "buying on mystery and selling on history" is generally correct. But often your mystery will, in effect, be someone else's history. This guide will point you in the right direction—toward building a well-balanced portfolio in what could be the best investment of the century, the North American or "penny" mining stocks.

Conclusions

1. Gold is still cheap. The current gold bull market will carry gold bullion prices much higher. But the real profits will be made in gold stock investments, especially where production is growing. North American gold mining is a dynamic growth industry. Several new exciting discoveries have already been made in the Hemlo region of Ontario and in the Carlin belt of Nevada. More will be made as explorations progress.

2. Whether a stock is cheap or not is a function of its market capitalization, not its share price. Market capitalization is determined by multiplying a company's share price by the number of shares it has on the market. A $1 stock with 100 million shares ($100 million market cap) is more expensive than a $10 stock with 1 million shares ($10 million market cap). Lower capitalization stocks, or "penny stocks," rise and fall faster than higher capitalization stocks. While most of the new production in North America will be by the higher capitalization companies, penny mining stocks will be the stocks that skyrocket.

2

Stages of a Mine

All mining companies try to be profitable, but few actually accomplish it. In the majority of cases, "mining" is a loose term, as most "mining" companies have neither an ore body (a mineral deposit that can be worked at a profit under existing economic conditions) nor a producing mine, nor will they ever. Gaining a better appreciation of the different stages in the evolution of a mine—and the relative degrees of risk attached to each—will aid investors in acquiring a diversified portfolio of mining shares that suits their particular investment temperament. Even among so-called penny stocks, there are "conservative" blue chips and flagrant crapshoots. Diversification begins by being able to tell the difference between the two.

Anything dependent on the price of a commodity—as mining shares certainly are—must be considered inherently risky, but there are still *degrees* of risk among mining shares. A producing mine's life span, cost of production, location, mining method, quality of management and many other factors define these risks.

In the earlier stages, before a mine has returned the cost of the project and is generating an acceptable level of profit, any piece of mineralized real estate must be termed a prospect—a mineral property the value of which has not been proven by exploration. Although prospecting and exploration are words often used interchangeably, technically, prospecting precedes exploration. While *prospecting* is the art and science of trying to locate mineralization that shows promise, exploration may best be defined as the practice of trying to finish what prospecting has begun. This concept of *exploration* applies to barren ground as much as it does to a long-life mine, whose continued lease on life depends on discovering new ore to replace spent reserves.

Prospects vs. Mines

While good prospects are hard to find, owing to the time and the number of competing interests in search of them, mines are an even rarer commodity. It is generally conceded that far more money has been spent searching for mineral wealth than has been extracted from the earth, but those instances that do pay off have been sufficient incentive for prospectors and miners for many centuries. Estimates suggest that only one prospect in 1,500 will yield adequate reserves of commercial-grade ore to justify the expense of going into production, i.e., becoming a mine. Ore bodies are indeed "accidents in the earth's crust." But before they qualify as ore bodies, such accidents are referred to as *anomalies*, areas that have different geophysical or geochemical characteristics from their surroundings. In rare cases, such anomalies may be explained by the presence of a mineral deposit beneath the ground. In even rarer cases, the mineral may be defined as ore.

Ore is an economic term, not geologic, and refers to *a mineral deposit from which a metal or metals may be extracted at a profit.* Depending on the price of the metal in question, today's ore can be tomorrow's mineralized rock. Improved recovery processes can also transform today's mineralized rock into ore. Other key variables that separate rock from ore are the type of ore and processing costs, the labor intensity of the mining operation and location of a deposit. Many significant discoveries in remote areas of the world, by their very remoteness, defy a profitable mining operation.

The Discovery Process

It used to be that gold and, to a lesser degree, silver were found in surface outcrops that often led to bigger and better things underground. Most such readily accessible mineral deposits have long since been found. The prospectors—and improved mineral-locating technology—of today have brought mining to a point where most of the biggest gold finds in recent years are actually invisible to the naked eye. (These are the Carlin-type disseminated deposits concentrated chiefly in Nevada.) Although mining has changed greatly over the years, the basic mining process remains much the same: mineral discovery leads to exploration, to development of a property's reserves and, finally, to a property's being put into production.

Once a valid claim has been secured, the claimants must proceed with a minimum amount of work on the property. This minimum, known as assessment work, is required on all unpatented mining claims (patented claims are those on which $500 has been spent and written title has been granted by the government). In order to show good faith and sincere intent to work the property, $100 worth of labor must be performed on each claim annually. The purpose of assessment work is to discourage the speculative holding of land and, more importantly, to encourage mineral development.

Stages of Exploration

After a property has passed the discovery test required for staking claims, the property must be further explored to define the extent of mineralization. It is at this stage that properties go from the prospecting phase into exploration. This exploration generally occurs in three distinct phases: geological, geophysical and drilling.

Geological sampling refers to the practice of physically surveying a property, sampling the rocks and analyzing the local surface features for evidence of mineralization. Geological evidence can be regional (occurring over a large area) or local (of limited scope). The age of rock relative to mineralization periods, the presence of favorable "host" rocks and other "pathfinder" elements and the presence of rock alteration are all pieces in what can only be called a puzzle at this point. Whether the pieces of the puzzle will fit together—and if so, the size of the puzzle—is a question that rock sampling and extensive mapping only begin to help to answer.

Once favorable locations have been outlined by traditional methods, geophysical methods are then employed. Geophysics is the study of the physical properties of the earth and, although many of the developments in this field have made great leaps thanks to recent technological advances, basic geophysical techniques go back many years. Seventeenth-century Swedish prospectors, who used magnetized iron bars to aid them in their search for iron ore, were the forerunners of today's computer- and laser-assisted geophysicists. Physical properties such as radioactivity, density, magnetism and electrical conductivity are clues that help isolate the presence of a concentration of mineralization. While geologic methods help to define the possibility of an ore body, geophysical methods help to confirm its existence.

Final confirmation of an ore body's presence is obtained

through diamond drilling. The drill bit is a hollow cylinder embedded with commercial-grade diamonds on one end and attached to a core barrel. The diamond drill secures samples that were previously available only in the course of actual mining. And because drill core samples contained values that could be determined and logged, the diamond drill contributed immeasurably to the expansion of minable reserves. Despite the wealth of knowledge that can be gained from drilling programs, the diamond drill is a tool that is sometimes better able to define geologic structure than to accurately assess the value of gold deposits.

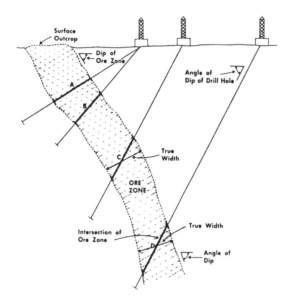

A section through a potential ore body showing its outline as inferred from four diamond-drill holes. By drilling in this manner, a three dimensional picture emerges from which an estimate of tonnage and grade can be computed.
Source: *The Northern Miner.*

Quartz outcroppings used to lead to underground gold deposits, before the advent of geochemical and geophysical methods designed to narrow down potential underground drill targets. Gold in quartz veins is usually so erratic that diamond drilling to establish reserves is usually not a practical method, as gold is among the most highly variable and erratic of mineral commodities.

At many mines throughout Canada, only one or two out of five diamond-drill holes that cut an ore body will show significant assays. One rule of thumb is that if 20 percent of the holes in a drill program "run" (contain gold), then there is a likelihood that the prospect is capable of developing into a mine. The erratic occurrence of gold also helps to explain the adage that "no mine is worth a damn until it's been turned down five or six times." The stories of ore bodies missed by inches and feet, or by drilling programs hitting waste rock within what subsequently proved to be significant ore bodies, are legion.

In many other instances, the inconsistent distribution of gold will yield spectacularly high results, often running into ounces and sometimes hundreds of ounces. This random variance is known as the "nugget effect," an abnormally high-grade section that cannot realistically be expected to extend throughout an ore body. Some promoters try to make use of such spectacular drill results, flaunting grab samples that are really selected samples and other incomplete data that serve their purpose in the marketplace. But at the same time, the company's geologists will be scaling down the assay to make it more representative of the whole deposit. This practice is known as "cutting" an assay. Erratically high values are cut, or reduced, to one ounce of gold per ton. One other common method of reducing assays to grades that are more representative of the deposit is to cut all high values to five times the average for the particular mine opening or deposit as a whole.

The intent is to be conservative at all times, because the decision to proceed or not proceed is entirely dependent on solid evidence that justifies continued spending. The rarity of ore bodies requires a degree of optimism from those who are so presumptuous as to think they might discover one, but optimism has no place in the sampling process. In rare cases where all values are high—in excess of one ounce of gold per ton—theoretically, no cutting is necessary. An exception where high values are not cut is in a sulfide ore body, where gold values are historically more consistent. The Hemlo gold camp, with its high sulfide ores, was an example of a consistent ore body with reserves that could be determined by diamond drilling.

At the exploration end of the business are the greatest risks—and also the greatest *possibility* for rewards. *Probability,* however, is what works against investors in exploration-stage companies. Still, the rewards that some-times come to those who finance the quest are what keep others coming in with new money. Making 1,000-2,000 percent on one's money, often in a short period of time, is all the incentive most people need.

The exploration-stage company is in many ways the most difficult type of company to evaluate. What—or whether—an exploration company has anything going for it is a question that's very much open to debate. That the de-bate is a highly technical affair at this point often doesn't leave investors with much basis for decision making. Initially, the geological phase gives way to geophysical work, which attempts to locate mineralized areas suitable for drilling targets; the drilling phase is the first point at which samples of what is underground are brought to the surface. If the news is good, the stock responds accordingly. As Morton Shulman wrote in *The Billion Dollar Windfall*, "...the market becomes a kind of lottery on each drill hole." A few good drill holes do not make mines, though.

And even when a "discovery" hole is followed by many more holes bearing commercial values, the initial excitement often gives way to boredom, as the formerly unknown becomes history and many investors take their profits and move on to the next speculative venture. Stocks "go up on mystery and go down on history." In those cases where good news does pave the way to lower prices, exceptional values are often found at vastly reduced levels of risk.

Because most junior companies lack the resources—both financial and technical—to take a property from the exploration stage into production, major mining companies often become involved after the junior has done the initial discovery work. In part because there are so many more of them, the juniors tend to find the mines and the majors tend to make them realities.

This phenomenon is especially pronounced in Canada, where small mining companies enjoy huge advantages over their American counterparts. Whether a company is Canadian or U.S.-based, joint venture agreements with majors frequently give a junior's stock another boost, as the willingness of a major mining company to spend money on a project often confers credibility in the eyes of the marketplace.

Developmental Exploration

After establishing that mineralization exists on a property and after drilling the property sufficiently to establish the existence of an ore body, the pure exploration company moves into the developmental-exploration stage. Developmental exploration will further define the ore body and provide the necessary data to formulate a mining plan. Concurrent with this more advanced stage of exploration is progress on the financial side. If the company has the ability to raise the money itself, usually only in the case of small projects or low-cost, heap-leaching operations, the company has either made arrangements for financing or is close to having finalized them.

If the company chooses not to place the property into production or cannot raise the necessary amount of money, a joint venture with a major would be likely at this point. Having discovered and partially developed an ore body, the junior is in a strong negotiating position by this time. The industry appreciates the rarity of ore bodies and also knows how much money is spent in search of them.

While financing and/or joint venture discussions are under way, drilling continues on the property. The object of this work is to outline the ore body, estimate and map the grade of the ore and classify reserves as either proven, probable or inferred tonnages. Without reserves, there is no mine. Determining reserves is an interdisciplinary effort requiring the involvement of geologists, mining engineers, metallurgists and even economists. The question all are trying to answer is this: How much metal is there in the ground and how sure are we that it exists?

The development of reserves is something that many mining companies try to rush along, but if they get too far ahead of themselves, they may find themselves with a mine without ore, or one that can't survive as predicted.

According to a recent article in *Mining Engineering*, when tonnages of ore or below-design-grade ores cause problems at a mine, "the mill blames the mine for delivering below-standard tons or grade and the mining engineer blames the geologist for overly optimistic assessment or incorrect interpretation of the deposit. The geologist blames the mining and metallurgy division for wrongly interpreting his data and conclusions, or simply fouling up a fine ore body."

Reserves can also work the other way around. Rather

than ore reserves being depleted before costs have been recovered, many large mining operations find themselves in the enviable position of expanding their proven reserves year after year. Homestake's mine in Lead, S.D., lists estimated reserves of 4 million ounces. The mine has been in production since 1876 and in recent years has been producing in excess of 250,000 ounces annually. Each year, new reserves replace those mined, a cycle that's common to world-class ore deposits, but not a routine occurrence enjoyed by most mines.

Reserves come in three types: *proven* (measured), *probable* (indicated) and *possible* (inferred). Proven reserves are those where the size, shape and mineral content of the deposit is well established from a closely spaced sampling. Probable reserves are based on less closely spaced samples and partly from projections based on geological evidence. Possible reserves are those for which few, if any, samples exist and are computed almost solely from geological evidence, as geologists and engineers try to gain a three-dimensional perspective of the ore body.

To understand the concept of ore grade, and to better appreciate its economic connotations, let's look at an example of "cutoff" grade—the lowest number (dollar amount) where mining and milling costs are equivalent to metal recovered (ounces of gold per ton). For instance, if it costs $50 to mine and recover gold from one ton of ore and gold is selling for $400 an ounce, the mine will lose money if it mines rock carrying less than 50/400 (0.125) ounces of gold per ton. This is the cutoff grade, below which the mine cannot operate at a profit.

The grade is an average that varies little; price, however, is a variable that spells the difference between ore and rock, profit and loss. Using the same example, computed at $300 gold, the cutoff grade would be much higher, 0.166 ounces of gold per ton. If the cutoff grade is lowered, reserves are increased at a lower average grade. And if the cutoff grade is raised, reserves build more slowly, but at a higher average grade.

The Metallurgy of Gold Ores

The mere existence of economic grades of gold mineralization does not ensure that gold can be extracted from its host surroundings. Different types of gold occurrence require different methods of extraction, which determine the cost of a mining project and ultimately dictate whether a mineral occurrence is indeed ore. The definitions listed below should take some of the mystery out of words you'll encounter throughout this book and, frequently, in releases from mining companies:

Oxide ores: Ore formed when minerals combine with oxygen. In the case of a gold-ore body, the oxidized zone would be that portion near the surface that was once subjected to weathering and the action of surface waters. Oxide ores are more amenable to heap leaching than any other type.

Sulfide ores: Ore in which the sulfide minerals, a compound of sulfur with more than one element, predominate. Metallic sulfides are usually insoluble in water and are generally found at depth in an ore body, where air and surface water have not altered (oxidized) the mineral occurrence.

Refractory ores: A refractory material is one that can be used at high temperatures; in the case of ore, refractory describes those ores that are difficult to treat. For example, gold sulfide ore must be roasted to reduce the ore to an oxide before the gold can be recovered. Refractory ores usually contain more than one metal.

The Feasibility Study

As ore is blocked out, tonnage estimates grow and grade estimates are made based on more samples, a company in the advanced stage of exploration commits to a feasibility study. This is a comprehensive work combining the efforts of the many disciplines involved. A feasibility study is the culmination of a long process of going from the unknown to the known and of numerous decisions to continue to spend money—rather than cut losses and move on to the next prospect. Preliminary judgments are made at many points along the way, but the feasibility study is the authoritative document that determines whether a project makes economic sense and is worthy of a positive investment decision. It is also a lighthouse of sorts, a comprehensive—and constant—reminder of the many facets of the operation that must be considered if the project is ultimately to become a profitable producing mine—and not wind up on the rocks. A feasibility study satisfies four main requirements:

1. It must indicate an expected rate of return.

2. It must show repayment and interest with the margin of profit on an annual basis.

3. It must provide the operating criteria (mining method, design, capacity) on which mining and milling operations are based.

4. It must be acceptable to banks or other sources of financing, as their participation will be contingent on a positive feasibility study.

The feasibility study is usually conducted by an outside engineering firm and evidence of such objectivity is highly desired before investing in an advanced-stage junior company. By this time, formerly highly speculative judgment calls now become quantifiable facts and risks; a rate of return must be projected and the mine's life determined. With this data in hand, the company can then sell a developed property; enter a joint venture with a major; issue stock in the United States, Canada or Europe; or secure alternative financing. It usually takes the developmental exploration company 12-18 months to start producing after the final feasibility study has been prepared and financing is in place. A company in this position is on the threshold of becoming a producing mine.

The Startup Company

Most investors confuse startup companies with producers. A startup company is one that has gone beyond feasibility and financing and is in its first year of production. Too often, startup companies are still spending consistently more money putting the mine into production than they are receiving from the mine. A year of production is usually required to determine if all the assumptions within the feasibility study were conservative or overly optimistic. Whatever can go wrong with a mining company will most assuredly go wrong during this first year, so good management and adequate working capital are essential to get through the crises that inevitably arise.

The variables over which there are no control are the market prices of gold and silver and whether those prices exceed the cost of production. The market never fails to remind us that ore reserves are dependent on the price of the metal being produced and that today's ore can be tomorrow's mineralized rock. Market forces determine whether a mine coming on stream will be a roaring financial success or an abysmal failure.

Production is the goal toward which all mining companies aspire, and commencing production during a period of high prices can pay for a mine in a couple of good

Sequence in Exploration and Development of an Ore Deposit

Stage	Type of Work	Possible Methods Employed	Costs ($ millions)	Risk
Exploration	reconnaissance	geological mapping, prospecting geochemistry geophysics, airborne surveys	0-5	extremely high
	initial follow-up	geological mapping, geochemistry, geophysics, limited drilling	1-0	very high
	detailed follow-up	drilling, limited metallurgical testing	4-0	high
	feasibility study	drilling, metallurgical testing, mine design, trial mining	10-0	moderate
Development	construction and mine development	site construction, drilling underground and/or surface mining	100-0	low
Mining	extraction & beneficiation of ore	various mining and concentrating methods depending on deposit	operating costs	low

Source: *Techniques in Mineral Exploration.*

years. Coming on stream during a long bear market often means struggling to stay alive.

Producing companies are those that have been in production for at least one year. The stock prices of such companies tend to reflect their investment-grade status and growth potential (both in reserves and in terms of annual production), and such stocks command much higher price-earnings multiples than their more hypothetical counterparts.

Producing companies should form the core of a mining investor's portfolio and are the base on which penny stock positions should be built.

More from Less: Heap Leaching

When one hears about the advances in technology that are changing the face of gold mining, chances are that the subject is heap leaching—not the introduction of Astroturf to the bottom of miners' sluice boxes.

Heap leaching, sometimes known as "solution" mining, is a centuries-old technique that was first devised about 1750 by Spanish miners who found that spraying piles of oxidized ore with an acid solution yielded copper. With a few modifications and some concessions to the environment, heap leaching of gold has been a growing sector of U.S. gold production, but not the almost obscenely profitable venture that some promoters of heap-leach properties would have a person believe.

The heap-leaching process owes its viability to improvements in metallurgical techniques and to the higher prices witnessed in the past decade. In conjunction with higher prices, and also in response to the trend toward depletion of higher-grade concentrations of gold, the U.S. Bureau of Mines and numerous mining companies began to seek solutions to the problem of extracting gold (and silver) from low-grade ores and mine waste material. They began looking at heap leaching, a process defined as the percolation leaching of piles of low-grade ores or mine waste that have been stacked on specially prepared pads to collect the solution bearing precious metals. The basic process of heap leaching dates back to the mid-1750s and, with refinements along the way, it has since been used to leach copper from open-pit copper mines around the world and also for the extraction of uranium from low-grade deposits.

The principle underlying the cyanidation process is that sodium or potassium cyanide, in solution with water, will dissolve gold (as well as silver) particles, thus releasing them from the surrounding rock. Lime is added to the water/cyanide solution to protect the cyanide from being destroyed by minerals called cyanicides. Because oxygen is required for the chemical reaction to occur, a weak cyanide solution (heavily diluted with water) actually attacks the precious metal particles faster than a strong solution.

As a chemical process for gold extraction, cyanidation was not introduced until about 1890. Cyanide leaching of heaps of low-grade gold ore was first successfully practiced by Nevada's Cortez Gold Mines in the early 1970s. By 1979, heap leaching accounted for 51,000 ounces of U.S. gold production. In three years, production by heap leaching increased fivefold to 250,000 ounces. In 1986, 998,603 ounces were recovered by heap-leach gold mines, 27 percent of overall U.S. production.

The Process

The process varies depending on the type(s) of ore being mined and the treatment required before cyanide solutions are applied to gold ores, but the basic process is this: Ore is stacked in heaps on impervious pads constructed on a slope.

Heaps are generally stacked 20-40 feet high and are then leached by turning on sprinklers that distribute the diluted cyanide solution over the ore piles. The solution percolates through the heap, dissolving the gold and silver, which runs out in solution into gutters at the edge of the heaps.

Heap Leaching

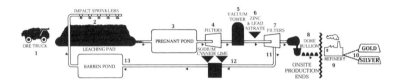

Source: Dean Witter Reynolds.

Crushing the ore prior to leaching usually improves recovery percentages and shortens the leaching cycle. It also raises costs, making some potential heap-leach mines uneconomic. Another step that is often necessary is agglomeration of the ore, the mixing of crushed ore with portland cement to bind fine ores together, thus assuring more uniform percolation.

The chief advantage of heap-leaching technology is the simplicity of the process. From the standpoint of mining entrepreneurs, the new technology, coupled with much higher prices, opened up a whole new vista of economically viable mining opportunities. Ore grades as low as 0.025 ounces per ton—1.25 ounces of gold in each 50-ton truckload—can be mined at a profit, versus conventional low-cost, open-pit grades of 0.15 ounces of gold per ton. Heap-leach operations, on the other hand, generally have significantly lower production costs.

High-grade deposits that individual prospectors or a

small work crew could mine using simple, inexpensive methods have largely ceased to exist. And as the grade of ore has decreased over time, the economies of scale associated with large mining ventures have dominated the mining scene. (The lower the grade, the larger the tonnage required to make a deposit economically viable.) The relative simplicity of the heap-leach process, however, has again allowed the small operator to gain a foothold in gold mining.

Capital costs for heap leaching are estimated to be about 20-25 percent of those for mines using a conventional cyanide treatment mill, and small heap-leaching operations can be put into production for less than $1 million. A 5-million-ton-per-year heap-leach mine could be put into production for approximately $10 million. Both figures are in sharp contrast to the average costs of $50 million (open pit) and $59 million (underground) required to bring a new gold mine into production. These figures come from a Metals Economics Group study, "Successful Strategies for Gold Exploration and Development." This study also reveals that, on average, four years elapsed from the time an operator entered a project until a production decision was made and another 15 months until milling began. Again, the much shorter lead time required for heap-leach mines—generally one to three years until actual production begins—gives these operations more flexibility in hitting the market cycle correctly. The payback period is also shortened and, therefore, the need for debt is reduced. Furthermore, with lower capital investments, the return on capital is usually greater than with a conventional gold-mining operation. It varies from one project to another, but it is safe to say that heap-leach gold mines are generally much better situated to withstand a prolonged period of depressed gold prices.

Heap leaching has its strengths, but among its weaknesses must be included a lower rate of recovery, usually 60-80 percent of the gold that is present. The gold is recovered in leach cycles as short as four to 12 days, or as long as two or three seasons of leaching. Conventional mill treatment usually recovers 90-95 percent of the gold. A grade of 0.1 ounces of gold per ton is a loose rule of thumb that dictates whether heap-leach or conventional recovery methods are employed. Grades below 0.1 are usually more amenable to heap leaching; higher grades usually justify other methods. But, as in all metal extraction processes, the goal is the highest recovery for the lowest possible cost; in short, the optimum gold recovery.

Aside from reduced rates of recovery, heap leaching is often fraught with metallurgical problems that require both time and additional milling processes to free the gold from the ore. A body of technical literature and more than a decade of experience have made heap leaching much more of a science and much less of an art than it used to be; but still, the mineralogy of the ore will determine whether or not the heap-leach method will yield the desired result: a profitable gold mine.

Conclusions

1. The greatest risk, highest potential rewards, price volatility and lowest prices are found in exploration-stage companies. They are best suited to traders and others in close proximity to the market. These stocks tend to be drilling "plays," and as such are subject to extreme price movement—both up and down.

2. Developmental-exploration companies entail much less risk than when they were pure exploration plays, but in view of the price decline that often sets in following positive exploration results, these stocks sometimes require a great deal of patience. Still, the best values—and most reliable prof-

its—are often found in this group and they are best purchased six to 12 months before they attain startup producer status.

3. Startup producers are often in a "wait and see" position, and the prices of such shares often will reflect the problems encountered during the first year of production. When startup companies have established themselves as producers, their shares suddenly gain respectability, a much higher profile among investors—and higher prices to match.

3

"The richest mine can always be found in the purse of a fool."

Old saying among Vancouver stock promoters

The Penny Mining Stock Markets

Mining stocks have a history of congregating in specific markets, each with a singular personality that distinguishes it from other markets where mining stocks are traded. Spokane, for example, is a haven for silver stocks, most of which have seen several cycles come and go. Denver is another true "penny" market, known more for a cyclical deluge of new issues rather than a market populated by veterans of several previous cycles. NASDAQ is a more accessible market than either Spokane or Denver and also requires a level of maturity and financial stability that would be the exception in those historical centers of mining-stock activity.

The Canadian markets—Vancouver, Toronto, Montreal and Alberta—are different still, distinguished by a greater number of companies and much greater ease of access to the capital markets. Vancouver is North America's foremost venture-capital market; Toronto is Canada's investment-grade exchange and a hotbed of companies entering the realm of gold production; Montreal and Alberta are lesser exchanges, each with a distinct personality and an enlightened, receptive outlook toward resource finance.

This latter point, an enlightened, receptive outlook toward the needs of small resource companies, is the primary factor that distinguishes small Canadian mining companies from their counterparts in the United States. The business is sought in Canada and actively discouraged south of the border in the United States. Canadian and U.S. mining companies may be on the same continent, but in many respects they are worlds apart. Several factors are responsible for the sharply contrasting mining-stock markets in Canada and the United States and for my own distinct preference for Canadian companies:

• While both countries developed in an east-to-west progression, driven by the discovery of natural resources, Canada's economy today is more dependent on natural resources than is the United States.

• As a result of this greater economic dependence on resources, the regulatory environment in Canada looks more favorably upon the raising of venture capital. In Canada, the regulatory climate favors resource development; in the United States, the regulatory climate makes it exceedingly difficult for the small mining company.

The greatest boon to the Canadian mining industry has been the phenomenon of flow-through financing, a form of tax-advantaged investment that has accounted for the vast majority of exploration funds raised by Canadian companies in recent years. The ready availability of funds for minerals exploration has given the Canadians a huge advantage over their American counterparts and is directly responsible for the existence and, indeed, the survival of many Canadian companies. Between proposed changes in flow-through rules and other changes in Canadian tax laws, this program is expected to be phased out beginning in 1988.

"We have been successful in establishing a venture capital market that no other world exchange can match."

**Gerry Fabbro
Chairman, VSE Board
of Governors, at annual
meeting, June 1986**

Vancouver

Vancouver, British Columbia, is home to the Vancouver Stock Exchange (VSE), the world's foremost venture-capital market and a study in contrasts of equally worldclass proportions. Simultaneously, Vancouver is the best possible market and the worst: a welcoming beacon for venture capitalists and entrepreneurs; a safe haven for what are often referred to as "those Vancouver bandits"; the greatest concentration of high-potential companies to be found anywhere—and a market where "failure avoidance" should be foremost in any investor's mind. To better understand the contrasts between the forward-looking market of today and the market still burdened by a richly deserved reputation, investors must first appreciate Vancouver's past.

Founded in 1907 to finance western Canadian oil and mining ventures, the VSE has always been a speculative exchange. "Boom and bust" is the trademark of all resource-driven markets and Vancouver has been through several cycles over the years. But the biggest influence on the Vancouver market's current position was not a new mining camp or oil field discovery in western Canada, it was a scandal in the Toronto market.

In 1963, Texas Gulf Sulphur discovered the famous Kidd Creek ore body and a flurry of speculative activity centered on surrounding properties, among them one held by Windfall Oil and Mines. Windfall's stock rose from $.40 to $5.65 on speculation that a drill hole on Windfall's property had also yielded a significant discovery. The promoters did little to dissuade this speculation and, when it became apparent that nothing had been found, the stock went from $4 to $.40 in one day. The lack of timely disclosure was Windfall's sin, which was later dwarfed by the realization that insider trading of massive proportions had occurred based on Texas Gulf's huge copper/lead/zinc discovery. In response to these transgressions, a Royal Commission report likened the Toronto Stock Exchange to "a private gaming club" and recommended major reforms.

The result of these reforms marked the end of the penny stock trade in Toronto and many of the penny promoters headed west to ply their trade in Vancouver. Not incidentally, that also marked the beginning of a long dry spell for minerals discovery and development by Toronto mining companies. In the late 1960s and early 1970s, Vancouver was a freewheeling, relatively unregulated market (populated in part by many former Torontonians) that coped with the ups and downs of commodity prices and, in the early '70s, survived the election of the New Democratic Party (NDP) in 1974. The NDP's Socialist program set out to "clean up the abuses of capitalism" the party perceived as stemming from the VSE. The new government's response was to levy double taxation on mining ventures, harass the VSE and do everything within its power to cripple the mining industry. The NDP's reign was short, but the disincentives they put in place worked: Canadians began to look beyond the province and to the United States for properties. As a result, there are more U.S. mineral projects held by Canadian companies today than are held by U.S. mining companies. And, in addition to Canadian companies looking to the United States for properties, more and more entrepreneurs from the United States are looking to the Vancouver market for financing.

Trading Distribution on the Five Canadian Stock Exchanges

VALUE

Exchange	1986	%	1985	%	% Change
Toronto	$63,684,095,245	75.3	$44,196,506,129	76.5	+44.1
Montreal	15,982,738,911	18.9	10,553,267,022	18.3	+51.5
Vancouver	4,484,517,920	5.3	2,718,838,471	4.7	+64.9
Alberta	476,110,586	0.5	292,082	0.5	+63.0
Winnipeg	476,110,586	*	1,266,553	*	–56.1
Total	$84,626,018,310	100.0	$57,761,960,537	100.0	+46.5

VOLUME

Exchange	1986	%	1985	%	% Change
Toronto	4,906,702,130	49.7	3,298,482,113	47.6	+48.8
Montreal	1,095,878,078	11.1	643,265,072	9.3	+70.4
Vancouver	3,493,491,147	35.4	2,752,966,088	39.8	+26.9
Alberta	369,243,470	3.8	229,372,061	3.3	+61.0
Winnipeg	518,394	*	1,862,121	*	–72.2
Total	9,865,833,219	100.0	6,925,947,455	100.0	+42.5

*Less than 0.1 percent.

Nonresource Companies

As more businessmen have sought out the VSE for the unique role it plays as a source of venture capital, one other trend has surfaced in recent years: the growing role of nonresource companies. In response to the downturn in oil and gas and precious metals prices in the early 1980s, promoters in search of a product not in disfavor began to bring nonresource deals to market; the percentage of resource companies on the exchange has declined from upward of 90 percent to about 70 percent today. Whereas the word "Resources" or the more optimistic "Mines" used to be an almost standard part of any VSE-listed company's name, new listings today are just as likely to include the words "Technologies," "Industrial" or "Capital." Some of the more colorful examples of the trend toward market breadth are companies such as International Burgers, Bathrooms Beautiful Canada, Gospel Music Network and Jolt ("all the sugar and twice the caffeine") Beverage.

Many of these companies are sometimes referred to as "concept" stocks. And as concepts are often easier to sell than results, some of the nonresource companies have been among the highest flyers—and most controversial stocks—on the exchange. Companies such as Neti Technologies and Chopp Computers must be included in any list of high flyers. Placing a value on these companies is a function of the level of promotion surrounding the story and, ultimately, whatever the market can be convinced to pay for it.

In this nonresource sector of the VSE, where selling the sizzle (rather than the steak) is the norm, gains of 1,000 percent are commonplace. Even more precipitous declines are almost equally common. Some observers of the VSE view the promotion and volatility as danger signs that should serve as adequate warning to investors contemplating a speculative investment. My point of view is that these companies, like the resource companies that still comprise the majority of the Vancouver market, represent a concentration of speculative opportunity not found in any other market.

Vancouver's Role

Vancouver is a vastly more regulated market than it was just a few years ago, but it is still the most freewheeling market in North America. Some of Vancouver's critics lose sight of the fact that the VSE is a speculative exchange and makes no pretense of being an investment-grade exchange. These

Underwriter Track Record
First Half 1987

Firm	Number of Underwritings	% Change
Canarim	29	67.94
Continental Carlisle	18	54.29
Yorktown Securities	15	77.08
Pacific International	8	113.65
Georgia Pacific	7	147.17
Jones, Gable	7	109.12
McDermid St. Lawrence	7	54.75
C.M. Oliver	7	31.39
Union Securities	6	257.78
Brink Hudson	5	114.24
Osler Inc.	3	169.23
Levesque, Beaubien	3	29.52
Jefferson Securities	2	100.54
Midland Doherty	2	70.24
Haywood Securities	2	51.85
Loewen Ondaatji	2	2.46
Wolverton	1	320.00
Merit Investment	1	300.00
Odlum Brown	1	62.50
Davidson Partners	1	41.67
Dean Witter (Canada)	1	0.00

Total: 128   Average: 79.53

Source: *Vancouver Market Report.*

people seem willing to accept the rewards that sometimes accompany the highly speculative ventures the VSE specializes in, but when things go wrong, they prefer to blame the market rather than their own inability to accurately assess the market.

The VSE has always been acutely aware of its role as a facility for raising venture capital. In terms of the number of companies and the amount of capital raised, Vancouver is unique among world venture-capital markets. Nothing else even comes close. At the end of August 1987, 2,079 companies were listed on the VSE, 212 of them newly listed since the beginning of the year. The ease of listing in Vancouver and a concerted effort to expand the market beyond the borders of British Columbia are responsible for a heightened profile of the VSE in recent years.

Going Public in Vancouver

To a degree that sets it apart from all other penny mining share markets, Vancouver's specialty is creating public companies in the startup phase. With more than 2,000 companies listed on the VSE, it would seem to follow that listing requirements are not terribly onerous. The minimum listing requirements are as follows:

• The company must be managed by individuals who have expertise or retained knowledgeable consultants in the area of the proposed project.

• A minimum of $60,000 must have been expended on the company's assets.

• The company must have raised a minimum of $100,000 by way of "seed" capital and a minimum of $75,000 during its first public offering.

• It must have issued at least 250,000 free-trading shares to the public.

• It must be sponsored by a member firm of the VSE,

have an acceptable transfer agent and be in full compliance with the B.C. Company Act, the Securities Act and all other legislation that governs the company's activities.

The process of obtaining a listing currently takes about three months, short by any standards and a brevity unknown in the United States. The average cost of listing is $25,000-$100,000, again a fraction of what it would be in the States and, not incidentally, one reason so many U.S.-based entrepreneurs have sought out the Vancouver market.

Before a company's stock begins trading on the VSE, though, it must first establish itself as a private company. That usually means that a mining professional—or a group of them—locates what is believed to be a mineral prospect of some merit. He secures claims to and, in some cases, purchases property, whose ownership he then vends into the company. In a newly created company, the vendors of the property receive an "escrow" stock position of 750,000 shares for having brought the asset to the attention of the company. (If a company has been in existence for some time and has undergone a reverse stock split—for instance, 1-for-2—the escrow position, at 375,000 shares, is also halved.)

Just a few years ago, there were few restrictions on the sale of escrowed shares. "I got off my paper" was one of the sweetest phrases to be heard on Howe and Granville streets. New rules on escrow positions allow for the release of the stock only by authority of the stock exchange and then only after the company has shown evidence of work progressing on the company's mineral property. Escrow stock, rather the release of escrow stock, is the carrot the exchange holds out to companies to help guarantee that the public's money is spent in the ground.

But before the public's money gets involved, the people behind the company offer "seed" or "founder's" stock positions to "close personal friends, business associates and relatives" of the company's management and promoters. No more than 50 persons may be involved at this stage, as that number of shareholders distinguishes private from public companies. The first group of shares, the seed stock, must be sold at a price per share equal to, or greater than, $.25. At least $100,000 must be raised by this type of stock issuance and there is no restriction on the number of shares that may be sold in this manner. If there are too many and the market cannot absorb the selling pressure created from the issuance of "cheap" insider stock, some companies find it difficult to recover from the initial wave of selling and the subsequent disinterest in the market that often accompanies it.

Depending on the price of the initial public offering, the company's seed stock may be held in trust ("pooled") and released in stages by the company's stock transfer agent. If the seed stock was sold at prices of less than 50 percent of the company's first public offering (below $.50 for $.25 stock), the stock must be pooled, to be released over a period of time according to the following schedule:

- 25 percent of total on day of listing
- 25 percent three months after date of listing
- 25 percent six months after date of listing
- 25 percent nine months after date of listing.

In the U.S. market, founders' stock positions are subject to SEC Rule 144, which usually requires a two-year holding period.

The process just described is the conventional method of launching a public company. Another way of attaining the same result, but with perhaps less expense, is through a "reverse takeover." This strategy involves taking a control position in a "shell" company with little going on but an exchange listing. The company is then reshaped to the purposes of its new owners. The best example of a shell company reborn is Bronson Mines, an exploration-stage company that had met with little success in five years as a publicly traded company. John Woods, editor of *Stockwatch*, tells this story best:

On Tuesday, February 19, 1980, Bronson did something that often causes exchanges and other regulators in less-enlightened jurisdictions to frown, glare and generally drag their feet—it changed hands. Based on not much more than a promise to try and raise some new money, the shareholders approved a 1-for-2 share consolidation, a change of control and a name change to Goliath Gold Mines.

Under the control of the Hughes-Lang group of companies, Goliath was soon paired with Golden Sceptre Resources, another Hughes-Lang company, in a drilling project in the Hemlo gold belt of Ontario. Shortly after, the drilling struck paydirt.

Today, Goliath and Golden Sceptre are partners with Noranda Inc. in a major new mine, Golden Giant. The mine is expected to produce 330,000 ounces of gold annually and indications are that reserves are higher than that.

Adjusted for stock splits, the shares of Goliath (the former Bronson) and Golden Sceptre have risen from a low of $.30 in 1981 to a high of $94.50 in April 1987. By simply buying out and changing the name of the nearly defunct Bronson, Hughes-Lang was able to get an exchange listing for their drilling project without the hassles of registering a new company. At the same time, shareholders in a defunct company wound up reaping an astronomical 315-to-1 gain; $1,000 became $315,000.

Reverse takeovers such as the one involving Goliath Gold have been increasing on the VSE; in fact, they've been encouraged as an alternative to the mushrooming growth of new companies. Latching on to a shell that's already listed on the exchange gives old investors another chance and lets the new control group devote its attentions to the project rather than spend time preparing for a listing and waiting for many months for the paperwork to pass through the regulatory pipeline.

Because of all the activity with new issues and reborn old issues, Vancouver has a history of being a short-term market, where investors are inclined to take small gains and go on to the next deal. The brokerage community has a vested interest in this strategy and with no shortage of new stories in Vancouver, sticking with a stock for any length of time is the exception, not the rule.

The investors who adopt a short-term perspective on the market are sometimes derisively referred to as "flippers" or as having a "10/10 mentality." That's as in "10 days or $.10, whichever comes first." The tendency of Vancouver to be a short-term market is also why the role of research in Vancouver is different: by the time a report can be researched, written and printed, the local client is long gone. In such cases, "research" is simply another word for "history."

The market participants who hold stocks, rather than buy and sell them, tend to be the Americans and other foreign participants on the VSE as well as investors from the prairie provinces of Alberta and Saskatchewan. Promoters view the investors in these places as one big "dumping ground" for stock.

Methods of Financing

The most popular method of financing in recent years has been the private placement. Simply, a private placement is the issuance of treasury stock directly to investors already knowledgeable about the company. Thus, there's no need to prepare a prospectus.

Because stocks or bonds in a private placement are issued only to supposedly knowledgeable investors, a company can generally assume that these securities will be held for the long term and will not be thrown on the market at the drop of the hat. A long-term horizon for investors, and its stabilizing influence on the company's stock, is critical to a company's future attempts to raise money. After all, no one wants to give money to a company whose stock has just plummeted. Raising money on the open market leaves a company open to the whims of speculators and short-term traders.

Conclusion

1. Vancouver is a market unlike any other in the world. It is home to the world's greatest concentration of mining companies and an active venture-capital market whose opportunities are outnumbered only by its pitfalls.

2. In the final analysis, Vancouver is what an investor chooses to make of it. He can heed the warnings of previous investors, some of whom recall a reputation that Vancouver is much less deserving of today, or he can attempt to focus on the success stories so common to Vancouver and so much more uncommon to other markets. Based on the track record of VSE companies, and thanks in part to the large number of them, I think there's little question which market is host to the greatest number of opportunities for substantial gains.

Toronto

The Toronto Stock Exchange (TSE) is Canada's largest and most respected stock exchange. Like the New York Stock Exchange in the United States, Toronto is Canada's investment-grade stock exchange, the facility for trading in most of Canada's major companies, 1,180 of which were listed in late August 1987. The city is Canada's leading financial center and, with the advent of financial deregulation in Canada, Toronto is taking on the flavor of a truly international financial center. The Toronto Exchange has long been North America's leading gold market and, after London and Johannesburg, the TSE is the world's third-largest gold share market. In 1986, 57 companies produced in excess of 5 million ounces of gold.

Although it doesn't square with its current image, Toronto was also once the scene of a highly speculative mining-share market, not unlike Vancouver today, the wildly speculative western counterpart to the staid, established market in Montreal. In 1899, the Toronto Stock and Mining Exchange joined forces with the Standard Stock and Mining Exchange and in 1934 the surviving entity merged with the Toronto Stock Exchange. The TSE and the Ontario Securities Commission (OSC) took severe action following the Windfall scandal in 1964 and effectively closed Toronto's doors to all but the major gold mining companies.

On the heels of the Hemlo discoveries in 1982 and in response to the warm reception junior mining companies were receiving in Vancouver (business that could have been transacted in Toronto), in 1983 the TSE responded with regulatory changes that once again made it possible for junior companies to raise venture capital for minerals exploration. Unlike all the other Canadian markets, which work closely with the provincial regulatory bodies, the market in Toronto is closely scrutinized by the Ontario Securities Commission, the closest parallel Canada has to the Securities and Exchange Commission in the United States.

1986 Gold Production
Toronto Stock Exchange

Symbol	Companies Listed on the TSE	Ounces of Gold
AGE	Agnico Eagle Mines Ltd.	75,646
AIG	Aiguebelle Resources Inc.	26,557
AMX	Amax Inc.	146,000
ABX	American Barrick Resources Corp.	186,072
AN	Amoco Corp.	223,000
ASM	Asamera Inc.	59,422
BLG	Bachelor Lake Gold Mines Inc.	20,140
BMG	(A) Battle Mountain Gold Co.	259,000
BME	Belmoral Mines Ltd.	52,613
BDM	Blackdome Mining Corp.	29,807
BPC	BP Canada Inc.	22,540
BWR	Breakwater Resources Ltd.	57,092
CBJ	Cambior Inc.	51,554
CXM	Camindex Mines Ltd.	6,663
CRK	Campbell Red Lake Mines Ltd.	277,564
CCH	Campbell Resources Inc.	21,000
CLT	Cominco Ltd.	139,800
FCL	Corp. Falconbridge Copper	107,000
DML	(A & B) Dickenson Mines Ltd.	44,135
DM	Dome Mines Ltd.	137,023
ECO	Echo Bay Mines Ltd.	320,693
EST	Equity Silver Mines Ltd.	42,900
FL	Falconbridge Ltd.	62,800
GLC	Galactic Resources Ltd.	55,000
GYK	Giant Yellowknife Mines Ltd.	113,220
GLG	Glamis Gold Ltd.	25,387

Symbol	Companies Listed on the TSE	Ounces of Gold
HBM	(S) Hudson Bay Mining & Smelting Co. Ltd.	66,000
N	Inco Ltd.	58,000
IRC	Inspiration Resources Corp.	7,000
ICR	International Corona Resources Ltd.	35,000
KER	Kerr-Addison Mines Ltd.	43,415
KGM	Kiena Gold Mines Ltd.	72,694
LCA	Lacana Mining Corp.	50,000
LAC	Lac Minerals Ltd.	*479,264
LOV	La Societe Miniere Louvem Inc.	30,451
MFC	MFC Mining Finance Corp.	16,353
MUS	Muscocho Explorations Ltd.	13,952
NOR	Noranda Inc.	**337,091
NGX	Northgate Exploration Ltd.	81,473
ORO	Orofino Resources Ltd.	5,139
PAM	Pamour Inc.	110,849
PGU	Pegasus Gold Inc.	92,000
PDL	Placer Development Ltd.	331,000
QTR	Queenstake Resources Ltd.	5,701
QUE	Queenston Gold Mines Ltd.	2,066
RAY	Rayrock Yellowknife Resources Inc.	37,981
RGM	Royex Gold Mining Corp.	17,504
SE	Sherritt Gordon Mines Ltd.	26,000
S	Sigma Mines [Quebec] Ltd.	64,714
SJG	St. Joe Gold Corp.	293,490
SUM	Sullivan Mines Inc.	27,213
TEK	(A & B) Teck Corp.	86,289
TLE	Total Erickson Resources Ltd.	35,653
WGI	Western Goldfields Inc.	6,750
WMI	Westmin Resources Ltd.	43,964
WFR	Wharf Resources Ltd.	26,000
WCC	Whim Creek Consolidated N.L.	37,827
	Total Production	5,103,461
		(158.7 Tonnes)

*   Including production from the Page-Williams Mine.
** Including all production from the Golden Giant Mine.
Source: *MPH Consulting.*

While Vancouver, Alberta and Montreal are essentially self-regulated markets working closely with the respective provincial regulatory bodies, the TSE sets higher standards for companies seeking a TSE listing, scrutinizes trading more closely than other markets and is backed by the strictest securities laws in Canada, those of the Ontario Securities Commission. Thus, many Europeans, as well as others who have had bad experiences in Vancouver, won't even consider the purchase of a Canadian company that doesn't have a TSE listing.

In the minds of this group and even among those who haven't sought out the TSE because of a "bad" experience in another market, the Toronto Stock Exchange represents an implied respectability not widely enjoyed by Vancouver companies. A TSE listing, in the eyes of many observers, is a sign that a company has satisfied stiffer requirements than are demanded of stocks trading in other Canadian markets. The TSE is the only exchange in Canada that has an independent committee that passes on the merits of companies seeking a listing. Perhaps more important than the stiffer standards, a TSE listing usually means that a more active market exists for a company's stock. For all TSE-listed stocks, there are two ways of making a trade: manually and via computer. As in Montreal, Toronto employs specialists (designated market makers) who buy from inventory when there are no buyers and sell from inventory when there are no sellers. In addition to the specialist system, Toronto also has a trading system known as CATS (computer assisted trading system), which automatically matches buy and sell orders. Originally instituted in 1978 to facilitate trading in inactive stocks, approximately 40 percent of TSE volume now occurs on CATS.

All Toronto stocks not listed on the TSE are monitored by a quotation system regulated by the Ontario Securities Commission known as COATS (Canadian over-the-counter automated trading system). COATS is a quotation system that is a less mature equivalent of the NASDAQ system in the United States. It disseminates quotes and is a storehouse of trading statistics and other market-related information for public companies whose shares are traded in Ontario. Together, the specialist system, CATS, COATS and strict oversight from the Ontario Securities Commission are the chief reasons the Toronto market enjoys the highest degree of credibility and integrity of any of the Canadian markets.

Lest it be inferred that I'm handling the Toronto market's PR account, no discussion of Toronto would be complete without a mention of the Toronto OTC market, an almost wholly unregulated market that contains many good deals and many more bad ones. Rather than discourage investment in the good ones, my suggestion would be to have good cause to trust the judgment of anyone suggesting the purchase of an unlisted stock in Toronto. Short of such an endorsement, remember that unregulated markets tend to attract unregulated types, a stereotype that's true of too many Toronto OTC stocks.

From West to East

Early in the 1980s, the TSE formed a committee to make plans to recapture some of the business it had previously relegated to other exchanges, chiefly Vancouver. The TSE accomplished this by reducing its listing requirements and segregating junior and senior company listings. Based on the new rules, juniors must have 200 public board lot shareholders (at least 1,500 shares each if the stock trades below $1; 100 shares each if above $1), a somewhat subjectively defined "property of merit," an independent geologist's report outlining a specific work program and a minimum of $500,000 working capital or cash equivalents (or a like amount of assured financing) to carry out the program. Listing fees range from a minimum of $3,500 to a maximum of $15,000 for junior companies, also within the range of other exchanges. Producers and near-producers must meet more stringent requirements, among them three years of proven reserves, working capital or defined plans to finance the property to production and evidence of future profitability, usually satisfied by a final feasibility study. But the essential point is that the TSE is now seeking business it turned away just a few years ago, and it's coming in.

In 1986, 165 new companies were listed on the TSE; through August 1987, 130 companies obtained TSE listings. Approximately 50 percent of this group have been mining companies, many of which have gotten a start in other markets. The TSE represents added credibility in the eyes of the investment community, a higher market profile, improved liquidity and marketability of shares (which helps in financings and acquisitions) and greater access to the European markets. For these reasons and others, the TSE has been hugely successful at "skimming the cream" off the Vancouver market, listing the VSE's initial successes and removing most of the volume in the stock to the TSE.

Toronto also allows negotiated commissions, which is another advantage, but in stocks listed on more than one exchange, improved liquidity in Toronto also means getting more when you sell and paying less when you buy.

It used to be that when a Vancouver company developed a mine, the stock "graduated" to the Toronto. Now, however, the TSE is spiriting away the best companies long before they have producing mines. Offhand, I can think of three examples in the past 18 months when companies I had previously recommended benefited greatly from TSE listings: Roddy Resources rose by more than 300 percent in the four months following its TSE listing; Emerald Lake performed similarly in the year following the departure of its market to Toronto; and Viceroy Resources rose from $1.25 upon its listing to $25, 18 months later. Several other companies that I've recommended to my readers have underperformed this group, but they still enjoy more active markets and vastly improved liquidity than when they were in Vancouver.

The reason for this phenomenon is that there is little effort on the part of VSE market makers to ensure that the business remains in Vancouver. As is characteristic of a new issues market, the brokers move on to fresh stories; the companies, or at least trading in them, moves on to Toronto. As *Stockwatch* editor John Woods remarked in a June 1986 interview in *Penny Mining Stock Report*, "Toronto is effectively kicking out the underpinnings that the VSE has built up for itself between 1976 and 1983. It's possible that the VSE can keep taking them away, but in the long run, it would probably be healthier for the Vancouver market to be able to point to their trading board and cite the wonderful successes, rather than point 3,000 miles away to Toronto and list the companies that began in Vancouver and went on to build the market in Toronto."

There's no sign of this trend reversing, but one recent arrival in Toronto is Canarim Investment Corp. Ltd., British Columbia's leading underwriter of Vancouver stocks. Toronto's willingness to accommodate the more speculative end of the business has attracted Canarim, a firm that pioneered in that niche out west, and should only serve to heighten the competition and raise the interest level in eastern junior situations.

Conclusions

1. The Toronto Stock Exchange is both an investment-grade market and one that has begun to return to its more specula-

tive roots. The advantages of the TSE include improved liquidity, a higher profile and increased marketability of a company's shares and the all-important element of credibility.

2. A TSE listing doesn't confer success upon a company, but it does mean that a company has passed a tougher screening process than is applied in other Canadian markets.

The broader exposure of a TSE listing, numerous recent examples would suggest, should certainly be a consideration in the selection of junior mining stocks.

Montreal

Montreal is home to Canada's first "respectable" stock exchange and has been, until relatively recent times, the country's undisputed financial center. Montreal retained its investment-grade aura while conceding the lead in trading volume to Toronto in the first half of the century, but it was not until 1976 that the blue-chip aura of Montreal began to emigrate to Toronto with a vengeance. The election of the Quebec separatist government at that time accelerated the exodus—of companies and people—to Toronto's Bay Street.

The stock market in Montreal had a brief fling with penny mining stocks in the mid-'70s but, after several stock frauds, decided to leave this business to other markets. Existing small Quebec resource companies found it almost impossible to raise money in the province and the Quebec Securities Act all but precluded the formation of new companies. From 1980 to 1984, only 11 new junior mining companies were listed on the Montreal Exchange. Most of the money that was being raised to explore Quebec properties was being raised across the continent in Vancouver.

In 1980, the Montreal Exchange hired an activist president, Pierre Lortie, who is largely credited with the innovative expansion of the exchange's product line and a new willingness to accommodate the financing needs of junior resource companies. (Not incidentally, in 1981 the Quebec Securities Commission amended its act to encourage junior companies to issue shares to the public.) The product line now includes gold options, platinum contracts and Canada's first 24-hour option market. If Toronto is most like the New York Stock Exchange, Montreal's stream of new financial products and newfound desire to accommodate resource finance makes it analogous to the AMEX exchange in the United States.

As president of the exchange, Lortie's biggest contribution, however, was his role as chair of a committee to recommend tax revisions to the federal government, changes that were designed to encourage minerals exploration and pass along tax incentives to Canadians willing to fund such programs. While the Quebec government had already adopted flow-through tax incentives in 1980 (allowing 166.6 percent deductions for minerals exploration, the most generous in all of Canada), the federal government implemented the 133.3 percent flow-through deduction program in 1983. Its effects were immediate and profound: 15 new junior companies were listed on the Montreal Exchange in 1984. In 1986, 40 new companies obtained listings, and exploration spending in the province increased 56 percent from the year before. In terms of new listings and exploration spending, the pace is well ahead of that in 1987. More important, the Montreal Exchange is participating in the activity in its back yard, not simply sending business to another market across the country. As a result of the trend reversal in Montreal, since 1982 the Montreal Exchange has more than doubled its share of the market for stocks interlisted in Toronto and Montreal.

Currently, the exchange's listing policies occupy a middle ground between the TSE and the VSE. Companies must have a minimum net working capital of $250,000, with 200 public shareholders holding a minimum of 500 shares each, a plan of exploration and a report from an independent geologist or mining engineer. The resurgence of activity has resulted in a scaling back of the additional 33.3 percent write-off enjoyed by Quebec-based purchasers of flow-through shares, but it has also resulted in a broader array of opportunities for those who wish to invest beyond provincial borders.

From a market standpoint, the exchange has offered increased liquidity to investors whose stocks also trade on other exchanges and, as in Toronto, a designated market maker system with a specialist assigned to every stock. Thanks to the innovations of recent years, it also has stocks in which to make markets.

Conclusion

The Montreal Exchange has rebuilt its venture-capital market in recent years, adding increased liquidity to dually listed stocks and active, two-way markets to Quebec-based exploration companies. As a result, the province has gone from being a dormant asset to a hotbed of exploration activity, producing both new mineral wealth and opportunities for stock market investors.

Alberta

Founded as the Calgary Stock Exchange in 1913 and officially becoming the Alberta Stock Exchange (ASE) in 1974, the stock market in Alberta has been driven by oil development. Through several boom-and-bust cycles, the ASE has been the center of the trading in publicly owned companies exploring for oil and gas. Originally founded in response to the Turner Valley oil boom, the ASE has been primarily an oil market over the years. Then known as the Calgary Stock Exchange, the oil share market went through three boom-and-bust cycles between 1914 and 1936.

In 1947, Imperial Oil's discovery of oil in the Leduc field brought the market back to life, sparking five exceedingly strong years ending in 1952. During this period the overall regulatory climate was lax to nonexistent, the volume of trading rose by 2,000 percent and Calgary was truly the Wild West. In 1955, the exchange enacted some badly needed regulatory reforms, but it was not until 1967 that meaningful regulations—modeled on those governing other Canadian markets—were adopted. Today, the market is largely self-regulated, with the Alberta Securities Commission and the ASE working together to regulate securities trading.

In the 1960s, further discoveries of oil were made in the Rainbow Lake region of Alberta, in the Mackenzie Delta and in the Arctic Islands and Beaufort Sea. The Alberta market boomed once more during the late '70s and early '80s. But, with the decline in energy prices and a worldwide recession under way, the Alberta market's greater dependence on oil stocks made it more vulnerable than most markets—and the volume of trading and share prices suffered accordingly. In 1983, the decision by the Toronto Stock Exchange to recapture some of the speculative end of the market prompted the ASE to ease its own listing process. The Alberta government, in an attempt to attract new business to the province, encouraged this policy, and so-called nickel pools have been the predominant story at the exchange ever since.

The nickel pools were modeled on the blind pools popularized in the United States and were essentially the same type of investment vehicle: a "shell" company with no apparent assets other than management, a minimum investment of $30,000 and the proceeds from a public underwriting. Perhaps even more than in the other markets requiring greater substance of prospective public companies, the typical Alberta new issue is truly a case of betting on the jockey, not on the horse. Because these companies lacked assets and an operating track record, they came public in the $.05-$.10 range; because there was really nothing to scrutinize, they could be processed quickly and cheaply. Companies not in the process of a public financing or seeking a transfer from another exchange can be listed in four to five weeks, with only 10 weeks required for a standard listing. The cost of a listing ranges from a minimum of $3,000 up to as much as $15,000, comparable to the other Canadian exchanges. Many of the junior oil and gas companies get an ASE listing first, in hopes of it later being a stepping stone to the Toronto Stock Exchange.

The relatively fast and loose listings policy has been a source of controversy, most of it stemming from a trading scandal in 1986 that resulted in the bankruptcy of First Commonwealth Securities. The firm's president and six others were arrested for stock manipulation involving Audit Resources, one of the early nickel deals that are now referred to as "junior capital pools." But despite the disagreements on the advisability of the junior capital pools, the number of new listings continues to grow: 139 new companies were listed on the ASE through July 1987, compared with 118 new listings in 1986. Of this group, 86 were junior capital pools, 14 were industrial companies and 39 were resource listings.

Conclusion

As in Vancouver, Alberta's closest counterpart among the Canadian exchanges, the variety of listings has broadened in recent years, but the exchange remains true to its roots: the ASE remains predominantly an oil and gas exchange. In view of the absence of fundamentals associated with many of the recent new listings, investors must be even more vigilant than usual when considering the purchase of ASE-listed penny stocks.

U.S. Over the Counter

Over-the-counter securities are those that don't trade on a stock exchange but rather are traded between brokerage firms on behalf of their clients. The NASDAQ (National Association of Securities Dealers Automatic Quotation) system is part of the OTC market, as are the "pink sheets," a daily listing of stocks with listed prices and market makers. To better appreciate the OTC market, let's first look at how a stock trade occurs on a U.S. stock exchange.

The investor first phones his broker and requests a quote on Homestake, a NYSE-listed gold stock that's been listed there since 1879 (one of only five companies listed at that time that remain on the exchange). The broker punches out Homestake's symbol (HM) on his desktop computer terminal and the quote appears on the screen. Homestake is trading at $47\frac{1}{4}$-$$47\frac{3}{8}$ and the investor tells his broker to buy 100 shares.

At this point in the transaction, the broker contacts his in-house trading department, who then contacts the exchange. A "runner" delivers the order to the Homestake post on the trading floor, to the "specialist" who makes a market in Homestake shares. The specialist's function is to maintain an orderly market in a security. Stock specialists own seats on the exchange where they make markets in a stock, and they make their money buying and selling for their own account, specifically, on the "spread" between the bid and ask prices. Stocks sold on an exchange are sold to the highest bidder, which makes the exchange an auction block market overseen by specialists who trade in the stock of individual companies. The price of the stock is a function of the specialist's interpretation of supply and demand for the security in which he maintains a market. Supply and demand will ultimately govern prices, but it is the specialist who sets prices in response to market forces—but only in those stocks that trade on a stock exchange.

Stocks not listed on a stock exchange are said to trade in the over-the-counter market. Of all the securities trading in the United States today, only about 5 percent trade on a listed stock exchange. Unlike an exchange, the OTC market is not a place but a way of doing business. Rather than specialists who maintain a market in a stock, OTC stocks have market makers who perform the same function. There are more than 6,700 securities dealers in the United States today, all overseen by the National Association of Securities Dealers (NASD), and these dealers agree to trade and maintain markets in specific stocks. In agreeing to that, a firm is guaranteeing to buy or sell a minimum number of shares at all times, which ensures that there is always a market for the security. Most stocks have more than one market maker, so liquidity is enhanced and pricing is competitive.

NASDAQ

The NASDAQ system came into being in 1971. Simply, NASDAQ is an electronic marketplace that accesses the prices posted by all of the firms making a market in a stock. There are more than 4,700 stocks in the NASDAQ system and an average of eight market makers per stock; there are as many as 30 for some of the more popular stocks. To qualify for a NASDAQ listing, a company must have at least 100,000 shares held by at least 300 shareholders, a minimum of three market makers in the stock, assets of

$2,000,000 and agree to file annual and quarterly reports with the SEC.

Because of the way the NASDAQ system has revolutionized the trading of OTC stocks, many companies that meet the stiffer requirements of the New York and American Stock Exchanges choose to stay in the OTC market. Multiple market makers, low listings costs relative to the exchanges and a relatively small amount of paperwork have made it an appealing place to stay, even for those firms qualified for listing on a major stock exchange. Most of all, though, NASDAQ has made it easy for investors to follow stocks for which prices used to be much more difficult to obtain.

One area of the OTC market where it is still relatively difficult to obtain quotations is in the "pink sheets," the daily publication of National Quotation Bureau, Inc. Known as "the pinks" (they've always been printed on pink paper), each day these pages list the bid and ask prices of upward of 21,000 securities. The prices are phoned in each day by market makers who are obliged to trade in the stocks. As in other markets, the market makers buy at wholesale (the bid) and sell at retail (the ask). The once-a-day quotes in the pink sheets are sometimes accurate for thinly traded stocks, but to make a trade, the trading department of the brokerage firm is required to check with at least three of the market makers listed in the pink sheets, then negotiate a trade with the market maker offering the best price.

While NASDAQ is a computerized market that any broker can access on a desktop terminal rather than phone around for the best price, the pink sheets require that the market be shopped for the best price. Prices among pink-sheet dealers sometimes vary a great deal, and buying at the lowest possible price can mean a substantial number of shares—and dollars—if a broker doesn't know anything about the market in an OTC stock. Paying "a few cents more or less" begins to run into real money. The wide variations in price, especially when dealing with a broker who doesn't specialize in penny mining shares, also help make a strong case for NASDAQ-listed issues. In Denver and Spokane, trading is done through the pink sheets and, to a much lesser degree, through NASDAQ.

The greater accessibility of NASDAQ stocks makes a strong case for stocks listed there, the theory being that any time the buying audience can be expanded, it's all to the good. The pink-sheet advocates would no doubt counter that limiting one's purchases to NASDAQ means missing out on the price appreciation that often precedes the greater degree of respectability required by NASDAQ.

Spokane

Among U.S. investors, Spokane is probably the penny market most people think of first. The Spokane Stock Exchange has been in existence since 1897, which helps to account for this familiarity, and it remains the only mining exchange still in operation in the U.S. today. The track record of Spokane during the period 1960-68—when the *average* listed stock rose by 15,700 percent—also explains why Spokane is so well known. Advertising copywriters have made liberal use of this statistic and even more liberal use of this one: Coeur d'Alene Mines went from $.02 to $20, turning a $1,000 investment into $1 million. As might be imagined, the Spokane market has been at a loss for an encore ever since the heady days of the 1960s. Today, the local penny market rises and falls on the price of silver and survives on the geological uniqueness of Idaho's fabled "Silver Valley."

The Silver Valley is a 25-mile-long, four-mile-wide stretch of Bitterroot Mountains that's been producing upward of 40 percent of the nation's silver for all but one of the past 75 years. In 1986, the mile-deep underground mines of the Coeur d'Alene (CdA) district occupied four out of the top 10 spots among U.S. silver producers, yielding 9.2 million ounces of the 32 million ounces produced in the United States.

The CdA district is one of only a handful of mining districts in the world where silver is the primary metal produced. The district's high-grade mines have been the beneficiaries of a unique geological phenomenon. Whereas most of the world's silver production occurs as a byproduct of open-pit copper mining and most of this silver is usually exhausted at depths of 400-500 feet, the vertical folding of the earth's surface in the CdA has produced mines with

Top 10 U.S. Silver Producers in 1986

				Production (million troy oz.)	
Mine	**Operator**	**Location**	**Mine Type**	**1986**	**1985**
Troy	ASARCO	Montana	U	4.08	3.64
Galena	ASARCO	Idaho	U	4.00	4.10
Coeur	ASARCO	Idaho	U	2.74	2.63
Candelaria	NERCO	Nevada	O	2.67	2.30
Escalante	Hecla	Utah	U	2.27	2.44
Delamar	MAPCO	Idaho	O	1.73	1.27
Tyrone	Phelps/Dodge	New Mexico	O	1.51	1.30
Lucky Friday	Hecla	Idaho	U	1.32	4.74
Sunshine	Sunshine	Idaho	U	1.15	4.71
Paradise Peak	FMC	Nevada	U	1.09*	0.00*

U = Underground   O = Open Pit   *Started production April 1986.
Source: *Spokane Journal of Business.*

exceedingly long lives. In terms of historical production, the CdA has produced $4.8 billion worth of metals through 1986, more than any other district in the history of the world. Another example of the CdA district's richness is historical production at the Sunshine mine. In operation since 1884, the Sunshine mine alone exceeds the total production of all the mines in the famed Comstock Lode. The district's silver mines weave miles of underground workings and currently operate in excess of one mile underground.

The Market

The mining-stock exchange that began in 1897 still operates in Spokane today. The exchange was created to facilitate trading in the mining stocks that sprang forth from the mineral wealth of British Columbia and northern Idaho. Although gold was the first metal discovered in what became known as the Coeur d'Alene mining district, lead, zinc and copper also were in abundance. But then as well as now, silver was the real story and most of the local companies are penny silver stocks.

Of the 43 stocks on the Spokane Stock Exchange, all but a handful are mining companies. The average company in this group is approximately 50 years old, in sharp contrast to the fast pace of new issues out of Vancouver and other mining-stock centers. In 1985, admittedly a slow year, there were no mining financings in the local market. In 1986, there were $10.5 million of local financings, approximately half of them junior mining companies. In fairness to Spokane, it should also be noted that Nelson Securities underwrote Inland Gold and Silver, a $.50 initial public offering trading at $2.50 just six weeks later. But this is an isolated instance and Inland's initial listing on NASDAQ only underscores the parochial nature of the Spokane market. Another local company, Pegasus Gold, the hugely successful heap-leaching pioneer, raised its public money in Vancouver, not Spokane.

Just as many companies that get their start in Vancouver "graduate" to trade in Toronto, the major silver mining companies of the Coeur d'Alene got their starts as penny stocks in the Spokane market. Although major stocks such as Hecla, Sunshine, Callahan and Coeur d'Alene Mines retain their listings in Spokane, virtually all of the trading in these stocks takes place in New York markets. Coeur's $.02-to-$20 track record has already been mentioned, and another striking example of the pennies-to-dollars meta-morphosis is Hecla Mining Co.'s flagship mine, the Lucky Friday: this worldclass deposit could have been purchased at auction in 1936 for $12. Today Hecla, largely on the longevity of the Lucky Friday, commands a market capitalization in excess of $550 million.

One way to judge the viability of any market is to track trading volume, and doing this reveals just how small the Spokane market is. Because trading figures are reported only for exchange-listed stocks, making it easier to follow a stock's price action, some observers of the Spokane market suggest sticking with listed stocks and avoiding the 115 issues trading in the local OTC market. But that's also where an estimated 75-90 percent of the trading activity takes place.

Because there are listing requirements for getting on the exchange and staying there, the local OTC market is dominated by companies that bring to mind Norman Lamb's remark: "Old mining companies never die, they just go on trading in the Spokane OTC market." This market is the over-the-counter equivalent to the "pink" sheets published daily by the National Quotation Bureau. Largely in deference to the market's long history, Spokane is the only market functioning in this manner today. Brokers for buyers and sellers of these stocks don't go to the pinks to shop the market in Spokane stocks, they go to Spokane. This quirk is one reason that many of you may have had great difficulty getting Spokane quotes from conventional brokerage firms. And if brokers can't get a stock's price on the screen on their desk, they aren't interested in buying it. Sometimes even their trading departments haven't a clue how to get a quote on most Spokane penny stocks.

The relative inaccessibility of the Spokane market is scheduled to change, as automated trading will make the 43 exchange-listed stocks available to all electronic quotation systems. Although the market will be more accessible, it still won't make up for the lack of fundamentals associated with most of the local stocks.

Many of the stocks on the exchange and in the local OTC market are typified by large spreads between bid and ask prices, with spreads of 50 percent or more not uncommon. This characteristic is even more pronounced in the over-the-counter market and poses very real problems for the person who decides to buy but fails to consider that he might someday wish to sell. The bull market track record of these stocks suggests that buying in bad markets will prove to be a good market for long-term investors, but Spokane can rarely be called a good trading market, even under the best of circumstances. It's easy to buy these stocks, but sometimes very difficult to sell them—especially all at one price.

Wide bid/ask spreads, the thinness of the markets in so many of the local stocks and frequently wide variations in price among market makers has produced a market that calls for patience in buying as well as selling. Months go by when some of the stocks don't trade a share and a broker's knowledge of this market is crucial to investors who insist on purchasing these stocks. Spokane is a market best suited to "nibbling" purchases, not the aggressive buying that can be absorbed by other markets.

Close Your Eyes or Analyze?

The random-walk approach to the penny mining market, recommended by Norman Lamb and others, evolved from the heady days of the 1960s. Then, silver doubled in price and the biggest stock market boom up to that time roared almost through the end of the decade; what can only be described as a market mania reigned in Spokane. To trot out an overworked statistic, the average Spokane stock rose by a multiple of 157. And, even if you didn't own Coeur d'Alene Mines as it rose from $.02 to $20 between 1960 and 1968, you didn't do too badly with the *average* gain of 15,700 percent. Similar gains have not been experienced in subsequent bull markets, however, and a look at the price histories of many Spokane-listed and OTC stocks reveals that the majority reached all-time highs in 1968. Despite the runup to $50 in the price of silver, the 1968 previous highs of most Spokane silver stocks remain intact. My attitude has always been that if $50 silver couldn't make these stocks hit new highs, I'm not sure what's likely to make that happen. Even so, many other stocks experienced gains of 500-1,000 percent during the last bull market. (More recently, as silver rose from below $6 an ounce to a short-lived high of $11.25 in April 1987, many of the Spokane penny silver stocks rose by 300-400 percent and have given back about half of their gains since then.)

If ever there was a market suited to the random approach—close your eyes, don't analyze—Spokane is it. It's also the market that first comes to mind when advisors such as Doug Casey say "Nobody knows anything, and therefore everyone is on an equal footing." (Actually, Doug hasn't said that for a long time and even Norman Lamb himself doesn't buy stocks that way.) Nevertheless, and kind as the random approach has been to previous generations of investors in Spokane stocks, I believe it still makes sense to make some concessions to geology, management and trading activity. In Spokane, the likelihood of exploration dollars being spent on a property is pretty remote. Remember, you're looking for a run for your money and you're not likely to get it from stock in a company with $500 in the bank, inactive management and 50 acres of moosepasture. That's an accurate description of many Spokane stocks but, as in previous bull markets, a lack of fundamentals isn't likely to stop their prices from rising.

Because "the ground is gone" in the Coeur d'Alene district, investors are not faced with raw prospects to choose among, but with an array of companies that have been in existence for many decades. Many of them will be around for many more decades, as unchanged in the future as they have been in the past. As I've indicated, the Spokane market is more about history than about the future, but there are still some ways to isolate opportunity there today. Perhaps the best way to narrow down the list of possible choices is to stay close to existing mines and previous producers. The following map marks the location of the mines (and former mines) of the Silver Valley. The light and dark lines mark the Osburn and Placer Creek fault lines.

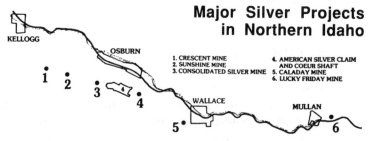

Major Silver Projects in Northern Idaho

1. CRESCENT MINE
2. SUNSHINE MINE
3. CONSOLIDATED SILVER MINE
4. AMERICAN SILVER CLAIM AND COEUR SHAFT
5. CALADAY MINE
6. LUCKY FRIDAY MINE

The theory behind this method of selecting companies in the district is that mineralization will be found beyond current and previous producers, at which point deals will be struck to allow mining to continue onto property held by another company. Companies frequently mentioned that fall into this category of geological coat-tailing include Abot, Atlas, Sterling, Consolidated Silver, Metropolitan and Allied Silver.

Buying next door to a current or former mine, sometimes referred to as "closeology," certainly increases one's chances of eventually owning shares in a penny stock success story, but it's still a bet made largely on the unknown. In most other markets, companies are selected on their individual merits, a combination of management and the amount of money they have to spend on minerals exploration or acquisition. In Spokane, where only a small amount of money is being spent on exploration in the district, stocks are often chosen based on what company A may do or discover and what effect that event would have on the value of company B. The phenomenon of buying next door to a mine in hopes that the known mineralization will prove to run onto another company's ground strikes me as akin to moving to West Los Angeles and praying for annexation by Beverly Hills. While proximity is clearly one way to increase the chance of success with a Spokane penny stock, it has little to do with fundamentals—and underscores the point that most of the companies in the district don't have control of their own destiny.

Conclusions

1. The unique geology of the Coeur d'Alene mining district is responsible for the longevity of the Spokane market and the silver producers of Idaho's "Silver Valley"—and all but precludes penny-stock success stories there today. In most cases, bets on Spokane stocks (and "bet" is the right word) are wagers on hysteria again taking over the precious metals markets, not speculations predicated on the possibility that a company will discover an ore body and develop it to production.

2. The Spokane market lacks liquidity, most of the stocks that comprise the market lack fundamentals and, while automated quotations can only help to make the market accessible to investors, informed investors are likely to seek out markets where a run for one's money is more likely to be found.
3. If $50 silver didn't make the stocks of Spokane exceed the highs posted in 1968, what will? The next few years may supply an answer to that question but, in the meantime, my advice is to be exceedingly selective in Spokane or, in most cases, ignore Spokane in favor of other markets.

Denver

Gold was discovered in Colorado in 1850 by Lewis Ralston while leading a party of gold-seekers to the Mother Lode of California. But not enough gold was found to keep them in Colorado. The Ralston party continued on to California and it was not until 1859 that gold in quantity was found and a true gold rush began in Colorado. Prospector William Parsons captured the essence of this particular gold rush:

> It was a mad, furious race for wealth, in which men lost their identity almost, and toiled and wrestled, and lived a fierce, riotous, wearing, fearfully excited life; forgetting home and kindred; abandoning old, steady habits; acquiring restlessness, craving for stimulant, unscrupulousness, hardihood, impulsive generosity, and lavish ways.

In short, your basic gold rush. "Pikes Peak or Bust" was both slogan and epitaph, as approximately half of the goldseekers perished crossing the plains toward "the new El Dorado" in Colorado. Many of the prospective miners who did arrive in the Rockies were farmers so green that it was said they "mined with pitchforks." With mixed results, gold was mined from placer operations surrounding Denver; eventually, mineralized "float" was followed into the mountains to the gold-bearing veins themselves. In 1865, a "silver mania" overtook the Georgetown area. But silver proved difficult to extract and it was not until 1868 that a smelting process was developed and put into operation in Black

Hawk and silver became economically viable to mine.

Whereas gold prompted the initial rush to Colorado, the decade of the 1870s was truly a silver decade. Production of silver rose from 496,000 ounces in 1870 to more than 11 million ounces nine years later. A discovery was made, production began, peaked out and mining district after district was left behind for the next strike. And there were many: Caribou, Georgetown, Leadville, Creede, Aspen and others spawned the rags to riches to rags story of Baby Doe Tabor and the Unsinkable Molly Brown (so named because she survived the sinking of the Titanic).

Labor disputes and stock manipulation schemes dimmed the fortunes of silver miners in the 1880s. But once again mining rallied. In 1890, the Cripple Creek gold field was discovered. This district was home to the Cresson mine and its fabulously rich "gold room"—one of the most concentrated gold finds ever. (To limit access to this particularly high-grade portion of the Cresson, a vault door was installed underground to prevent theft.) With the resulting rush to Cripple Creek and later collapse of the silver market, gold again displaced silver as the dominant metal mined in Colorado, a position of preeminence it holds to this day. Uranium had its boom—and bust—in the '50s; oil and gas stocks were the dominant players in the '70s; precious metals stocks materialized once again in the late '70s and the '80s.

The Denver Penny Market

Because Colorado's economy was founded on resources and still relies heavily on mineral production, a speculative stock market has existed almost from the initial discovery of gold. Since the resource markets topped out in 1980-81, the Denver market has been preoccupied with high-technology stocks—and just about any new venture seeking risk capital. Unlike Vancouver, there is no formal Denver Exchange: the market is simply a loose association of underwriters of new issues. The stocks trade over the counter in the United States.

Because Colorado has a tradition of being a center for capital formation, initially for mining ventures and today for all manner of penny stocks, the state has liberal securities laws and no merit review system that determines the worthiness of new issues, sometimes better known as IPOs (initial public offerings). Approximately half of the 50 states require only that a new issue meet the SEC's disclosure requirements. Others have more stringent requirements and thus many new issues often can't be purchased in some states. Traditionally, those with the most stringent requirements are California, Iowa, Wisconsin, Arizona and Texas. States most receptive to new issues include Florida, New York, Nevada and Colorado.

Despite the relative ease of listing a company in these states, in recent years the underwriting community in Colorado has resurrected a form of financing that was widely used in the 1920s. Known as "blind pools," these are public companies without a product or a business plan; their stated goal is to devote the proceeds of the underwriting to the acquisition of a business. The formalities, costs and lengthy registration process of the SEC, the proponents of blind pools argue, account for their popularity. Whereas it can often take up to a year to complete an initial public offering, blind pools can become public vehicles within a matter of weeks.

Because the goal of all blind pools is unstated, investors who purchase them are betting solely on management's ability to use the proceeds of the underwriting in a way that will justify a higher price in the aftermarket. In 1985, all U.S. blind pools—many of which were launched in the

Denver market—rose by an average of 234.6 percent, outperforming all other initial public offerings selling for $5 or less. In 1986, the trendiness of blind pools had diminished, partly in response to an SEC opinion letter hindering their access to the public market. Although performance figures aren't available for blind pools in 1986, one expert estimates that they fared about half as well as they did in 1985.

As for Colorado-based penny mining stocks, Denver has a track record of presenting opportunities for profits but has few stocks that have demonstrated staying power. In addition to requiring that investors be highly selective, in recent years investors haven't had many choices in the Denver market: there was only one mining deal brought public in 1985 ($368,500 was raised in a real estate deal that happened to be located on some mining claims). In 1986, there were only three mining deals, so the penny investor looking for mining deals in Denver has few to choose from. The Denver market also has a track record for mining deals to give one pause.

Many of the companies on the table on page 74 were among a group dubbed the "Scintillating Sixteen," a name derived from their performance earlier in the decade. With few exceptions, there's little that looks scintillating about many of them today. As the table demonstrates, selectivity in Denver is crucial. (Rather than paint all of the Denver market with the same brush, some notable exceptions to my bias against Denver stocks would include Silver State Mining, U.S. Minerals Exploration, Crown Resources, Canyon Resources and Horizon Gold.)

In fairness to Denver, a similar indictment of Vancouver mining issues could easily be constructed. The difference that makes Vancouver preferable, in my opinion, is that there are more than 2,000 companies in Vancouver and a mere

Metals and Mining Issues from Colorado Underwriters

Company	Underwriter	Shares	Offering Price	Capital Raised ($ millions)	Effective Date	6/18/87 Bid
American Gold Minerals	E.J. Pittock	8,000,000	$.50	4,000	11/5/80	n.a.
Cripple Creek Gold	C.E. Carlson	2,500,000	.20	500	9/14/87	n.a.
Equity Gold	M.S. Wien	3,000,000 [1]	1.00	3,000	9/25/80	n.a.
E.R.I. Gold & Silver	J.J. Krieger	15,000,000	.10	1,500	7/28/80	.05/.15
Lake City Mines	Wall Street West	6,000,000	.25	1,500	12/31/79	n.b./.10
Moritz Mining	Seaboard Planning	750,000	.8333	600	10/3/80	.01/.10
Silver State Mining	S.W. Devanney	15,000,000	.10	1,500	12/17/79	2.57/2.63
U.S. Minerals Exploration	J. Daniel Bell	20,000,000	.10	2,000	7/10/80	6.50/6.75*
Apache Energy & Minerals	N. Donald; Int'l Sec.	8,000,000	.25	2,000	6/11/80	.01/.03
Colorado Gold & Silver	G.S. Omni	30,000,000	.10	3,000	9/3/81	.01/.04
Franklin Consol. Mining	J.J. Krieger	3,200,000	.15	276	11/3/77	1.00/1.125
Gold Ore Ltd., Cripple Cr.	Wall St. West	20,000,000 [2]	.25	4,000	5/11/81	n.b./.03
Grayhill Exploration	J. Daniel Bell	33,000,000 [2]	.10	3,300	12/21/81	†
Intermountain Resources	Security Traders	6,000,000	.25	1,500	1/26/81	n.b./.04
Marathon Gold Corp.	Wall St. West	6,000,000	.50	3,000	11/12/82	.28/.31
Saratoga Mines Inc.	C.E. Carlson	20,000,000	.10	2,000	12/24/81	n.a.
Sierra Resources	Blinder, Robinson	2,000,000 [2]	.50	250	12/20/77	.16/.18
Crown Resource Corp.	Chesley and Dunn	8,000,000	.50	2,000	8/23/83	.46/.53
Golden Gate Minerals	Vantage Securities	40,000,000	.025	1,000	6/13/83	n.b./.01
Goldsil Mining and Milling	Wall St. West	10,000,000	.50	5,000	10/28/83	.10/.15
OMX Corp.	First Financial Secs.	30,000,000 [3]	.05	1,500	7/22/83	n.a.
Canadian Minerals	Dillon Securities	16,000,000	.10	1,600	1/6/84	n.a.
Leadville Silver & Gold	Blinder, Robinson	24,000,000	.075	1,800	2/10/84	.05/.20
Mallon Minerals Corp.	First Interwest Secs.	2,650,000	1.00	2,650	1/6/84	.31/.34
Syracuse Minerals	Atlantis Sec.	15,000,000	.05	750	6/1/84	.02/.03
Western Int'l Gold & Silver	Mills Fin'l Services	60,000,000 [2]	.02	1,200	3/7/84	n.b./.0075

*Reflects 5-for-1 stock split. [1]Merged into U.S. Minerals. [1]Units made up of two shares and one warrant. [2]Units made up of one share and one warrant. [3]Units made up of one share common, one Cl.A Warrant and one Cl.B warrant.

Source: *The Denver Post/Irving Hale.*

handful in Denver. Denver's abysmal track record for underwriting mining deals stands out because there are so few of them; in Vancouver, the sheer number of winners obscures the many that have fallen by the wayside. Among other notable differences between the two markets, Vancouver has a formal stock exchange with more or less consistent prices. On Denver's regional over-the-counter market, however, wide spreads between bid and ask prices are commonplace and, as has been true since the early days in Colorado, it's still easier to raise money on penny stocks than on those that sell at higher prices. As a result of the Denver market's distinct preference for stocks selling literally for pennies, the local stocks also tend to have large numbers of shares.

With large amounts of stock out, it is often difficult to post big advances in the price of a stock and when it does happen, the resulting high market capitalization is often difficult to justify. Other than taking a very specific approach to the Denver market, my feeling is that it's also difficult to justify the purchase of most of the local mining deals.

Conclusions

1. Denver is a market characterized by a small number of mining deals, highly capitalized companies and an undistinguished overall track record. There is no formal exchange and the companies trade over the counter with wide and variable bid and ask prices.

2. In spite of the drawbacks, some excellent companies have emerged from the Denver market. As in other markets, choosing management with care is the best way to ensure that you will own a stock that proves to be an exception to my admitted bias against the Denver market.

Australia

I have never visited Australia and my direct experience with Australian stocks is limited to one (it was a disaster). Between this limited experience and observing several "put another investor on the barbie" stock promotions in the early 1980s, it's fair to say that I have not been enamored of Australian gold stocks.

More selfishly perhaps, there's no shortage of good deals in North America, and Vancouver, with its 2,000 mining companies, is just a two-hour plane ride away. Sydney, on the other hand, is a 14-hour trip and there are only about 470 companies on the Resource Board, approximately 80 percent of them mining companies, most of these concentrating on gold.

There are also increased logistical problems associated with doing business there. Many of these securities trade in three different forms (and at different prices). These include fully paid shares (similar to a common share in the United States or Canada), partially paid (requiring an additional future payment by the investor) and options on the fully paid shares. For trading simplicity, U.S. investors should concentrate on the fully paid shares.

These are among the reasons I lay no claim to expertise in Australian gold stocks, fully aware that some of my concerns apply to me as an advisor and not necessarily to you as individual investors. Whatever my own reasons for a lack of experience in Australia, they don't negate the considerable opportunities available to investors in the Land Down Under.

There have been three distinct gold rushes in Australia. The first got under way in 1851, when Edward Hargraves found gold at Summer Hill Creek, New South Wales. Hargraves named it Ophir, after the biblical city of gold. It's possible that Hargraves also had Ophir, Calif., in mind, as he had only recently returned from the California gold country, where a latter-day Ophir is located. Hargraves' discovery of gold in Australia occurred because he noted many similarities between the rocks and geological setting in California and his adopted homeland. While most mineral discoveries of that period were fortuitous events, the discovery of gold in Australia was the result of deductive logic and applied experience.

Having learned the basics of placer (streambed) mining in California, Hargraves returned to Australia to test his theory. With two local farmers, he set out to locate gold on the tributaries of the Macquarie River. The group met with early success and Hargraves received a substantial reward, was made a commissioner for lands and was later presented to Queen Victoria for the key role he played in the development of Australia's mineral wealth. (Technically, gold had been discovered before Hargraves, but news of it was suppressed because it was feared that the predominantly convict population would get gold fever and lose all control. In another instance, a farmer's workmen building a water-race for a flour mill discovered gold. The farmer quickly convinced them it was mica; he preferred raising wheat to the prospect of mining gold—and having a stampede result from the news of its discovery.)

Hargraves, in contrast, told the story of his discovery far and wide. A gold rush to New South Wales resulted, which later spread to Victoria and then to Queensland. Australia's second major gold rush took place in western Australia in the 1890s, with most of this growth occurring on Kalgoorlie's "Golden Mile." Exploration here resulted in the discovery of the famous Mt. Charlotte mine and several other long-lived producers were later developed nearby.

The Current Gold Rush

Gold production in Australia has grown at a faster pace than in any other country in the world, up a whopping 342 percent from 1980 through 1986. At 75 tonnes, Australian gold production is gaining fast on its historical record of 119 tonnes, set in 1903. By 1989, Australia is likely to overtake the United States and Canada as the western world's second-largest producer, behind South Africa. There are several good reasons for this most recent Australian gold rush.

As elsewhere, the historically high price of gold makes gold mining highly profitable in Australia, where the average cost of production currently approximates about $200 (U.S.) per ounce and is in steady decline. Seizing upon an exploration trend first developed in the southwest United States, the Australians have in recent years discovered gold at a rapid pace, as evidenced by 20 new gold mines now slated to come on stream by 1990. About 90 percent of these mines are low-cost open-pit operations, in contrast to the previous deep underground operations that followed narrow, discontinuous veins and in which it was notoriously difficult to develop reserves. Applying heap-leaching technology to old mine dumps and to lower-grade ores passed over by previous mining has also helped add to Australian production. The carbon-in-pulp recovery process is another new technology that has also contributed to rising Aussie gold production. The Australians have even developed some gold extraction technologies of their own, chief among them the coal-oil agglomeration process.

In 1987, Australia enjoyed an appreciating currency relative to the U.S. dollar. The result is that Australian gold mining companies have received more U.S. dollars for their gold. In short, Australian gold mining companies have had the best of both worlds: expanding gold production and a higher price for their product. Currently, the Australian dollar trades for $.70-$.75 (U.S.). Many analysts believe the Australian dollar will continue to strengthen against the U.S. currency if there is a resurgence in the price of resource-based commodities.

While much of the depreciation in the Australian dollar would appear to be in the past, there are several other advantages enjoyed by Australia that account for its rising gold production—and the Australian Gold Share Index's spectacular 75 percent increase between January 1 and the April 1987 top in gold stocks. Outside of Canada, the United States and South Africa, Australia is really the only other choice for the gold-share investor. And with much of the institutional money shunning South Africa, Australia is suddenly more attractive to large pools of capital seeking a haven in gold stocks. In late 1986, the low P/Es relative to North American gold stocks made Australian gold stocks look very inexpensive, a condition enhanced by suggestions that a gold mining tax would be imposed.

The prospects of a tax on gold mining hung like a dark cloud over the Aussie gold stocks into December 1986, at which time it was announced that any tax would be shelved. In response, the Aussie shares took off. Aside from the postponement of the gold tax, the Australian golds were already trading at much lower multiples than their North American counterparts. Today, the average Australian producer is trading for approximately 25-30 times earnings, with the best-known North American producers trading around 60 times earnings.

To the institutional money that has just begun to discover the Australian market in the past year, the shares Down Under still look cheap. While most of the advances in

Australian stocks can be attributed to growing institutional involvement, individuals are also beginning to discover these stocks. They're also discovering that the Australian markets are different from the more familiar markets of North America.

Market Mechanics

There are six states in Australia and a stock exchange in each capital city. Together, these exchanges comprise the Australian Associated Stock Exchanges. About 90 percent of the overall volume takes place in the Sydney and Melbourne markets and all of these markets are subject to the same rules and regulations. Only a small number of stocks, generally the high-capitalization companies, trade in ADR (American Depositary Receipt) form; thus, a direct purchase of shares is usually required. Because of time and currency differentials, to say nothing of the general lack of information on Australian gold shares, it is imperative that investors deal with specialists in this market.

There are about 150 gold mining companies to choose from in Australia. Due to the unusually large number of projects coming on stream and the rapidly growing gold production of many of the established producers, my impression is that the penny market should be avoided by most people in favor of the more established companies. These are the companies that will be revalued by the market and, not incidentally, these also will be the companies that gold funds will be buying as huge sums of money flow into them over the next few years.

No discussion of Australian gold production would be complete without mention of the discoveries in the so-called "epithermal arc," an area of intense volcanic activity where

Top 20 Australian Gold Producers

Company	Project	1986 Prod. (ounces)
Placer Pacific	Kidston	239,231
Western Mining Corp.	Kambalda/Lancefield/Emu/Stawell	192,141
BHP	Ora Banda/Telfer	160,119
Kalgoorlie Min. Assoc.	Fimiston	131,995
Central Norseman	Norseman	109,884
Kalgoorlie Min. Assoc.	Mt. Charlotte	108,666
Jimberlana	West Wittwater/Pamour	107,333
North Kalgurli	Fimiston/Paringa	100,977
Peko	Mt. Morgan Tennant Creek	98,782
Renison Goldfields	Mt. Lyell/Pine Creek	86,247
Barrack	Horseshoe Lights/Wiluna	76,711
Sons of Gwalia	Sons of Gwalia/King of the Hills	74,173
Pancontinental	Paddington	70,914
Aust. Cons. Minerals	Golden Crown/Westonia	57,503
Carr Boyd Minerals	Harbour Lights	57,396
EZ Industries	Elura/West Coast Tasmania	54,918
Hill 50	Mt. Magnet	51,899
Whim Creek	Meekatharra/Bald Mountain (U.S.)	41,669
Endeavour Resources	Bluebird/Ingliston	40,098
Great Victoria Gold	Great Victoria	36,477

Total Australian Production: 2,336,187

Source: Frank Renouf Brokers Pty Ltd.

the largest gold discoveries in recent years have been made. One example of this offshore growth is Placer Pacific's Ok Tedi mine. Located in Papua, New Guinea, Ok Tedi produced in excess of 620,000 ounces in 1986, dwarfing all of the Australian mines—and Ok Tedi is only one of many large gold mines that will attain production in the next few years. Names like Lihir Island, Porgera, Misima Island and Vanuatu will become familiar names as they develop into some of the world's largest gold mines in the years ahead.

Conclusion

Gold production in Australia is growing at a faster rate than anywhere else in the world today and Australian gold stocks represent some of the best values to be found anywhere. But because of the specialized nature of this market, investors must do their homework—and seek the advice of people who specialize in Australian stocks.

4

*"When everyone
thinks alike, everyone
is likely to be wrong."*

Humphrey B. Neill

Penny Strategies

Not too many years ago, the prevailing belief among
investors was that penny mining stocks were little more than
a blind speculation on higher precious metals prices. In theory, and sometimes in practice, these stocks were to be purchased early and sold in stages into a rising gold market.
Ideally, investors in this inherently volatile field would obtain the outlandish rewards that are widely available in the
late stages of a runaway resource market.

The difference between now and then, however, is that
while previous markets were fueled on raw speculation and
mass hysteria, the precious metals markets of today are
predicated on what has become a highly profitable business
venture.

Gold mining and minerals exploration and development
companies can now be subjected to analysis, not reduced to
buying based on the slickness of the company's promotional
materials or your mother's maiden name, the way many
people pick horses at a racetrack. Or, for that matter, buying
penny stocks in Spokane.

Although higher precious metals prices have reduced
some of the inherent risks of exploring and mining gold,

silver and, more recently and to a much lesser extent, platinum, the search for and subsequent production of these metals is still a high-risk venture that is dependent on the price of the commodity being mined. For this reason, it is essential that investors are conscious of the risks that stem from fluctuating commodity prices.

High Risk and Long Term

Even though opportunities abound in the penny mining market at current price levels ($450—and higher—gold) and will still be widespread at substantially lower prices, it remains essential to understand that all mining stocks are at the mercy of the price of the commodity being sought, developed or mined. If the advisors predicting substantially lower gold prices are correct, this will have an extremely adverse effect on the prices of junior mining stocks. As a group, precious metals stocks are almost wholly at the mercy of future price trends.

Having said that and having previously stated my belief that the next few years will be a period in which gold prices seek much higher levels, I think the first thing investors must do is define their perspective before entering the penny gold markets. Aside from an appreciation that gold stocks are at the mercy of the gold price, having a well-defined point of view on the price trends of precious metals will help dictate both the degree of commitment and the timing of purchases and sales of penny mining shares. Having a philosophy on gold also makes it easier to take action at the appropriate time—or to weather the periodic price adversity that is common to all markets, sometimes especially so in the case of gold.

In addition to holding a point of view that both justifies an involvement in the market and reinforces investment decisions during those periods when they seem most in question, a point of view on gold also helps dictate an investor's strategy toward the penny market. An opinion on gold will likewise help to determine whether these stocks are held for the duration of a long bull market in precious metals, whether a trading strategy is adopted or whether these markets are avoided altogether. An opinion on gold will also determine how penny mining investments fit into the scheme of an overall investment portfolio. Most investors own no gold or gold-related assets. Others view gold solely as an insurance hedge and hold only a small amount of the physical metal. Still others view gold and gold stocks as a uniquely profitable sector of the larger market—and commit substantial percentages of their portfolio to it.

I've often been asked what percentage of a portfolio should be allocated to precious metals and to the penny mining stocks. Financial planners and others who allocate assets on that basis usually have an answer to that question, but I never have. It depends almost entirely on the person asking the question, his overall investment philosophy and its relation to current economic conditions and the investor's level of experience with the investment—whether it be gold, common stocks, junk bonds or rare coins. If an investor has found most of his success in one area and known failure in others, he should stick with what works best for him—and, I believe, be disproportionately invested in it as well.

Diversification

The subject of this book addresses only a small portion of most investors' portfolios. It concerns an inherently speculative niche—precious metals mining stocks—and is heavily weighted in favor of the most speculative end of that sector, the so-called penny stocks. These stocks are inappropriate for some investors, simply because their economic circumstances argue against the assumption of risk—the retired, for example, who live on fixed incomes and don't have capital to risk. That last part is important, as many retired people do have capital to risk and do quite well for themselves in the penny markets.

In many other cases where economic circumstances would certainly allow for the acceptance of higher risks in exchange for the prospect of greater rewards, the individual's temperament precludes taking risks. Many, myself among them, would argue that even higher risks are routinely assumed by some of this group and that perhaps many of those with the greatest aversion to risk would profit from a reconsideration of their opinion.

But rather than attempt to sway investors to my admittedly biased point of view (penny stocks have worked for me and thus I am disproportionately committed to them), I believe people should seek a comfort level and gain experience in the market. Based on that experience, the investor should work to develop a strategy that suits his financial and temperamental willingness to assume financial risk and, perhaps more importantly, squares with his own track record in the market.

Just as precious metals mining stocks represent a segment of a larger portfolio, penny mining shares should occupy only a portion of a broadly diversified precious metals portfolio. At its core, that portfolio should consist of gold and silver bullion and blue-chip producers. Like a pyramid rising from a base of security, more speculative issues should be added to a portfolio only after a conservative safety net is in place. At least some portion of the bullion is an insurance policy that should be held through thick and thin; beyond that "insurance" position, the metals should be bought and sold based on changing economic conditions. The blue-chip gold stocks, in my estimation, are best suited to profiting from cyclical advances in the price of gold. Some would no doubt argue that they, too, have a place in a "through thick and thin" portfolio.

The percentages represented by bullion, blue chips and penny stocks are highly variable and should be based on investment philosophy, temperament and previous experience in the market. I know people who very prudently have gold and silver coins and large portfolios comprised of the major North American gold producers, rounded out by a small speculative portfolio of the penny shares. The penny shares might occupy 10 percent of the overall portfolio invested in precious metals. This would be a traditionally "conservative" strategy. On the other extreme, I know many people who hold large percentages of their net worth in gold and silver mining stocks. I lean toward this latter category and think it's reckless not to be heavily committed to gold stocks at this time. Whatever the approach, it must be one that suits the individual's preconceptions about the market.

Within the context of a precious metals portfolio, penny mining shares should represent a diversified group of companies. Mining is a game of bad odds, and owning shares in numerous companies reduces some of the inherent risks of mining stocks while at the same time increases the probability of rewards. To complement the producing companies in a portfolio, most investors should own stocks from the nonproducing categories: exploration, developmental exploration, development and startup production. Those willing to accept greater risks for the prospect of greater rewards should favor the exploration companies; those who prefer the greater probability of rewards in more advanced projects should favor producers and near-producers. Personally, I lean toward the lower-priced stocks, simply because they have a track record of doubling and tripling with greater ease.

The allocation of assets is the most important decision

investors make. Betting the wrong way on a major trend can prove to be a costly mistake; betting right on the trend and buying the wrong stock can also be a problem. One of the ways to avoid being correct about the trend but wrong on individual stocks is to own several of them. However, I think owning too many stocks is a common error of investors. Under only a few circumstances would I recommend owning more than 20 companies, as it's difficult to have solid, well-informed opinions on that many stocks at one time.

When investors do own as many as 20 companies, I assume they have at least $100,000 in the market. For the investor with $10,000 to spend on a portfolio of mining shares, my suggestion would be to spend the money on four or five stocks and try to follow their activities closely. For investors who don't have the time to follow the market closely, especially if they lack experience in these markets, I would suggest more stocks, perhaps as many as eight or 10. Brokers make about twice what they would on fewer, larger trades, but an anticipated attitude of neglect argues for more, not less, diversification.

A Strategy for Profits

At the heart of any strategy designed to generate profits must be a system to limit losses. Capital preservation is essential, as that can spell the difference between being in and out of the market. Because having money to invest is *the* crucial component of any successful investing program, capital preservation is arguably more important than the prospects for price appreciation.

One of the reasons that maintaining your investment capital is so crucial to any strategy designed to add to that amount is the magnitude of the gain required to recoup a large loss. To illustrate this point, let's look at four examples:

% of Initial Capital Lost	% Gain Needed to Break Even
25	33
50	100
75	300
90	900

Too often, investors tend to enter the market *with* an awareness of the downside risks, but *without* a strategy to address these risks when they materialize. In the case of most stocks, I think the use of stop losses is essential. But where penny stocks are concerned, my view is that stop losses must be used with great care. Whereas one might allow a 10-15 percent margin for error in traditional stocks, my advice is to allow 20-30 percent with penny stocks. Their greater volatility requires a wider tolerance for error, but even when giving more latitude to penny stocks, the use of stops in the penny markets often means that investors are putting themselves at the mercy of people who come in with a "market" order to sell at an inopportune time, thereby causing a temporary price distortion. When this happens, their stock is liquidated as a result of someone else's igno-rance of the market, their tendency to panic or merely the willingness of someone else to move on to something else—sometimes almost irrespective of price. Whatever the cause, when this aberration is past, the market often quickly returns to its previous level. Too often, the use of stop losses results in selling when buying was in fact the more appropriate strategy.

The other reason I don't recommend the blanket use of stops is because, once stopped out, people tend not to get back into the stock. If the stock doesn't go right back up, they often tell themselves it's going lower; just as often, the adverse price movement poses questions that result in an inability to repurchase stocks that have just been sold, albeit in the name of capital preservation.

There are three times, I think, when it is probably wise to use stops: 1) when a trailing stop is employed to protect a substantial profit, 2) when a stop is used to protect capital when purchases are made following a big advance in price, and 3) when shorting the market. In the first case at least an acceptable profit is being locked in. In the other two the investor is protecting himself from himself when using margin or when a purchase is being made late in response to news or a promotional blitz. There's usually a fine line between "chasing" a stock and improved fundamentals justifying a higher prices. The goal, obviously, is to stay on the right side of that line.

Just as I think the use of stop losses is often ill-advised in the penny market, the pennies require another break with normal investing practices: averaging down in penny shares is usually not a good idea. Too often, especially with inexperienced investors, it only means that poor timing and perhaps poor stock selection are being rationalized—and that a mistake is being compounded. There are exceptions, but unless the investor is experienced, has done his homework or is following the advice of someone who has (neither method is infallible), adding to losing positions should usually be avoided.

Stop losses lend an element of protection to these sometimes blurry distinctions in a market where investors are often better off out of the market than in it. Stop losses represent the downside of buying a stock, and one of the best ways to avoid the need for stop losses is to get the market timing down right.

When to Buy

"When everyone thinks alike, everyone is likely to be wrong" is the essence of the contrary opinion investment strategy. Humphrey B. Neill, to whom the preceding is attributed, is generally regarded as the "father" of contrary opinion. The necessity of going against the crowd illustrates human nature at work. It is also an example of crowd psychology that drives home what is easily the most important tenet of investing: Go against the crowd and you will be right more often than you will be wrong. It is also why selling silver was a timely move in 1980, when the wily shrewdness and immense wealth of the Brothers Hunt were being heralded on the front pages of *Time* and *Newsweek*; and why their recent forced sales and bankruptcy filing can be construed as a buy signal. The advantages of buying at market extremes is even more important in the penny markets, because these stocks are so much more volatile than bullion itself. In the past year, gold has ranged from $378 to $482, a range of 27 percent. In contrast, the average stock of the 34 currently followed on my newsletter's monthly Scorecard has had a range of 320 percent in the past year. A contrary strategy rewards investors in any market but, because of the greater volatility of the penny shares, the rewards of true contrary investing are significantly more pronounced.

Seasonality

Aside from being contrary in the timing of purchases, which always maximizes the amount of stock an investor ends up owning, some times seem to be better than others to purchase penny mining shares. One quite reliable tactic has been to buy stock late in the year, as tax-loss selling sets into the markets in selected stocks. In fact, there have been many years when it has been exceedingly difficult to buy in December and lose money.

Stocks that posted their highs early in the year and trended down for the rest of the year are high on the list of the most likely candidates for tax-loss selling. These are followed by stocks that were unusually volatile—in both directions—throughout the year. In the case of stocks that hit their highs early in the year, I'd strongly question whether a stock that declined throughout the year is worth owning. "It's selling for so much less than it used to" isn't good enough; there has to be a good reason to believe the stock is now going to make the transition from winner to loser. In any event, stocks with a downtrending price history are the ones most likely to be subject to selling pressure late in the year. It's often a good idea to beat the rush and sell well in advance of the end of the year.

In those cases where a stock that's been in decline for most of the year still appears worthy of purchase, the most opportune time to do so is likely to be in November or December. As usual, one person's adversity is another's opportunity.

In addition to the annual phenomenon of tax-loss selling creating some unusually good opportunities to enter the market, the end of each month has been known to create similar downturns in the penny mining issues. In Canada, brokerage firms must settle their accounts at the end of each month, the net result of which is that positions are settled by liquidating stocks that have not been paid for within the required settlement period. This is generally more pronounced in Vancouver than in the other markets, as brokerage firms there seem to allow more latitude than is seen in the other markets. The stocks most susceptible to the month-end downturn are frequently those that have been flying high throughout the month, because these are the stocks in which investors have a tendency to overextend themselves as they try to ride the wave of excessive speculation.

When to Sell

So far, I've outlined defensive strategies for selling, advocating them only in the most limited sense. One strategy that I strongly advocate is the sale of stocks that have not performed to expectations. Expectations are, of course, what get investors into the market, and the absence of expectations is often ample reason to justify a sale. Usually, but not always, such stocks are losers (and in hindsight make a case for the use of stop losses). Sometimes stocks that haven't lived up to expectations just haven't moved at all and, unless there's good reason to think that's going to change soon, they should probably be sold. There's no shortage of good stories out there and when your money has been invested in a stock that's done nothing for a year or more, you should question if there's still a good reason to own it.

The inability of many investors to bite the bullet, whether it be with stocks that aren't working out or merely aren't ripe with the same expectations they were at the time of purchase, is the reason many investors end up owning 25, 30, 50 or more companies. These people buy companies and, rather than sell when things don't work out, relegate them to a kind of "nonperforming" corner of a portfolio. Like old clothes in a closet that they hope to wear again, some investors file these stocks away in hopes that they'll come back to life. Sometimes they do: Rea Gold is a stock for which I had low expectations, in part because Rea was down a consistent 70 percent from its purchase price two years earlier. My recommendation in March 1986 was to sell at $.65; a year later the stock went from $.55 to $9 over a four-month period. In this business you're always a drill hole away from looking like a jerk, but that isn't always reason enough to hold perennial losers—or those that are merely tying up funds that you're convinced would do you more good invested elsewhere. When you are convinced that your money is better off invested somewhere else, leaving it where you have low expectations is a passive adoption of a strategy that depends on a good market taking care of yesterday's mistakes.

There are a few perennial loser/low-expectation stocks in my personal portfolio and the reason I haven't sold them is that they represent so little money relative to my overall portfolio. But in those cases where a stock is tying up a meaningful amount of money that would be better off invested elsewhere, I sell that stock and buy one that appears more likely to produce a profit. Too often, investors go from *expecting* to make a profit to *hoping* to make a profit. It's this condition that is at the root of some very large portfolios. Realistically, it's tough to have well-informed opinions on 10-15 companies. On 25 or more, unless an investor is devoting huge blocks of time to the project and has a substantial amount invested in the market, there's little justification for this breadth of exposure and even less hope of being current on all of them. Furthermore, when you own that many companies, the relative differences tend to be more readily discernible, which helps distinguish which companies ought to be owned disproportionate to others—or not owned at all.

Up to now, this discussion of selling has addressed the defensive strategy of stop losses and the often more difficult prospect of dealing with stocks that haven't gone up or down—they just haven't done anything. Having dealt with the failure of stocks to live up to their initial expectations, it's time to consider what to do with those stocks that do rise in price. Like dealing with losers and laggards, what to do with winners is not always an easy decision.

The penny markets require that investors be contrary to ensure stocks are purchased at opportune times (when nobody else wants them) and sold when the news is good (and everyone else wants to buy). The markets in many penny shares lack liquidity much of the time and investors must take their liquidity where it can be found. This requires that stocks be sold into news and other events that generate buying in a stock, because often that's the only liquidity that's available in many of these markets.

It is generally conceded that it's easier to call a market bottom than it is to identify a market top. Gloom, it seems, has limits that can be defined. Euphoria and greed, on the other hand, often seem to know no boundaries. In the realm of profit-taking, perhaps even more than in defensive selling, it's crucial to have an individual strategy. There are conservative strategies, aggressive strategies, evolving strategies, flexible strategies and all kinds of various strategies, but in order to know what to do with a profit, it is essential to have a strategy of *some* kind.

Most people who enter the realm of penny stocks do so for the prospect of high, and occasionally outlandish, rewards. Personally, I expect to routinely make at least 200 percent on my money and, with some regularity, do much, much better than that. In a classic bull market, gains of 1,000 percent will almost be routine. My inclination is to own a stock for that kind of gain if I think it may be attainable. Other people may be satisfied with much less; the point is that a strategy should suit the individual, and there are innumerable strategies that can accomplish that goal.

Perhaps the most widely recognized strategy to lock in a profit is to sell half of a stock position if it doubles in price. As a money-management technique, this is a conservative play that I'm willing to concede may suit some people. I've just never been one of them. One of the reasons is that it has never squared with my admittedly more aggressive outlook toward these stocks and, not incidentally, because it would have cost me a great deal of money if I'd employed it. While

I do indulge my money in some exceedingly speculative pursuits, my inclination is to be an investor, not a speculator. It suits me and it works—and those are the two most important elements of any strategy.

The sell-half-on-a-double strategy is a sure way to instill mediocrity in a portfolio. My own preference is to work to isolate the best stocks in a portfolio, rather than to arbitrarily sell half of what may turn out to be a stock that should have been held for much larger gains. I recently came across a study by the New York Stock Exchange that further illustrates the perils of taking quick profits. This study focused on stocks that had risen in value by a factor of 10; a corollary study isolated stocks that had declined by a like percentage. What this study found was that the stock that went up by 1,000 percent had 27 changes of ownership along the way. Stocks that declined by the same percentage changed hands only twice on the way down. The people in this example, at least, were cutting short their profits and letting their losses run—exactly the opposite of the way it's supposed to be done.

One exception to my preference to hold for the long-term is when a "windfall" profit is achieved. In most of the cases I can recall when a stock doubled or tripled within a month or so of owning it, the smartest strategy usually was to have sold at least half. When almost immediate doubles and triples are attained, there are times when this means that the fundamentals justify buying more—not selling. But more often it means that a stock has gotten ahead of itself and could later be repurchased at a lower price.

How long investors choose to hold on to a stock should be a combination of many factors, not the least of which is price. It has always been my contention that low price is one of the essential ingredients of any definition of high potential. I'm not close-minded to the potential of higher-priced stocks, it's just that I lean heavily toward what one study characterized as the "theoretically inexplicable but empirically persistent phenomenon" of superior performance of low-priced stocks. Stripping this argument of its academic slant, this could just as easily be defined as the "hummingbirds can move faster than elephants" theory. A consideration of the top 10 performing stocks on the *Penny Mining Stock Report* Scorecard further illustrates this point:

Top 10 Recommendations

Stock	Recommended Bid	Current Bid*	% Gain
Viceroy	$.54	$C22.00	3,974
Roddy	.35	4.25	1,114
Perron	.52	5.12	884
Golden Knight	2.13	10.50	392
Emerald Lake	2.03	10.00	392
International Platinum	.95	4.50	373
Geddes	.96	4.10	327
Amir	1.07	4.50	320
Flanagan Mcadam	1.05	4.20	300
Goldstack	.74	2.80	278

*As of September 4, 1987.
Source: *Penny Mining Stock Report,* September 1987.

Six of this group of 10 sold for less than $1 when recommended and the average price was $1.03 (the average for the rest of the list is $1.60). Because a rising tide of precious metals prices tends to raise all the stocks, it's become very difficult to find stocks selling for less than $1 that possess strong fundamentals. Still, I feel strongly that low price is one criterion for high potential. It's also a helpful indicator to estimate how much profit you should expect from a stock. There's something to be said for $5 stocks, but they won't go to $25 as quickly as $1 stocks go to $5. Investors shouldn't expect them to and their strategy should factor lower expectations into the purchase and subsequent sale of higher-priced stocks. Investors must remember to always think in percentages, a practice that's particularly helpful as profits accumulate. The $1 stock that has already risen to $5, a gain of 400 percent, cannot in most cases be expected to duplicate the performance from $5.

Those who regard themselves as traders, not investors, would be obvious exceptions to my advice to ride profits rather than arbitrarily sell half of a position on a doubling in price. Aggressive though this strategy may be, I also recommend taking profits: at least partial profits have been recommended at various times in the top five stocks on the list above. Having owned two of this group, I can vouch for the practice of selling for 500–1,000 percent gains on occasion.

My belief is that expecting to at least double your money is not unrealistic. Of the 24 companies that have been recommended since June 1985 (when I began recommending stocks in *Penny Mining Stock Report*), one is even, two are down in price, one was deleted from the list at a profit and the remaining 20 are up in price. Of the 20 up in price, 15 of them are up by more than 100 percent. The point of this exercise is simply this: profits should come from your big winners, not your average stock. When the average stock is up by more than 100 percent, it doesn't make sense to me to base a profit-taking strategy on average performance. Profits are supposed to come from winners, not average performances. When the average stock is more than doubling, the investor's task is to isolate those stocks from which the greatest performance is likely to come.

Sell on a double only if it squares with a short-term trading philosophy or your own ultraconservative investment viewpoint. Profits are hard to argue with and, if you entered this market because you thought gold might again trade as high as $500, the sell-half-on-a-double strategy makes sense. But, if you think gold has a good chance of heading higher over the next couple of years, the sell-half strategy is shortsighted and will only cut into the greater profits that should instead come your way. Brokers like to encourage this strategy, as it usually means two commissions. "Nobody ever went broke taking a profit" is the adage that often accompanies this sage counsel. What they neglect to mention is that nobody ever becomes rich taking small profits.

Shorting/Margining/Retiring

Shorting—One of the reasons that Canadian mining stocks tend to be so much more volatile than their U.S. counterparts is that the market is played in both directions, just as it is in the U.S. commodity markets. Clients of Canadian brokerage firms can sell stocks (go "short" the stock) or buy stocks (be "long" in the market). U.S. investors with U.S. accounts cannot short stocks but can short the market through Canadian brokers.

This strategy is not for everyone; in fact, it's only suitable for those who are willing to watch the market closely, which invariably means working closely with a broker, both to limit risk and to maximize entry and exit points. Aside from margins being suitable only for some people, the various exchanges have strict rules on shorting and the individual firms have even stricter requirements. In Vancouver, for instance, VSE stocks qualify for shorting only if they have been trading for at least three months and clients must have a specific type of account: a "short" account that allows clients to sell stocks they don't own. (A short account also happens to be a margin account; more about that later.)

When selling short, the investor is betting that the price of a stock is headed lower and borrows the stock from his brokerage firm, with whom he must maintain a cash balance of at least 150 percent of the amount of the sale. That's for stocks selling for $2 and above, which, as the following chart demonstrates, is the most favorable of the short-sale margin requirements:

VSE Margin Requirements for Short Selling

Price of Security	Minimum Balance Required
$2 and higher	150% of market value
$1.50-$1.99	$3 per share
$.25-$1.49	200% of market value
below $.25	100% of market value plus $.25/share

Many firms don't encourage short selling and all recognize that the VSE standards are minimal and comfortably exceed them. Shorting is a trading tool that should only be used by traders. It is also an effective strategy for a bear market, but in the current bull market it may only be appropriate for those of you who are willing to actively follow the market and can accept the sometimes heightened risks of betting against it.

Margin accounts—Like shorting the market in a given stock, the use of margin is a trading strategy that entails more risk than an outright purchase of stock. It is unsuitable for those who are unwilling to shoulder the financial consequences of being wrong in betting on a stock's future price direction. Investors who buy and sell on margin post a margin requirement that will vary from firm to firm, depending on the preference of the firm. The exchange minimum requirements in Vancouver don't allow the use of margin on stocks selling for less than $1.50 and many firms don't allow the use of margin below $2. They tend to set their policies according to whether they want to encourage or discourage the practice within the firm.

Internal policies within firms will vary a great deal, but employing margin (again, only possible through Canadian brokers) is an aggressive strategy that should be used only by active traders. Used properly, it can be an extremely effective way to leverage your trading profits. Used improperly or in conjunction with imperfect timing, margin can also be a way to leverage an investor's mistake.

IRA, Keogh, etc.—Most everyone is familiar with the seductive ads that show how the miracle of compound interest will make a person in his 20s a millionaire by retirement age. What these advertisements don't show, and many investors never even consider, is that penny mining shares offer the prospect of reaching that goal much sooner. My experience with penny stocks in retirement plans has been positive and I've talked with enough of my subscribers to know that many of them have achieved some impressive gains with penny stocks in IRA, Keogh and other tax-deferred retirement plans.

Because of the "risks" associated with penny mining shares, I know there are many who believe that penny stocks and retirement programs are mutually exclusive propositions. If an investor's temperament allows him to take risks, and assuming he's not too old to recover from any mistakes he makes, taking some risk with at least some retirement funds is a strategy that should be considered.

Aside from the possibility of greater percentage gains than are generally available in other investments, there are other good reasons penny shares are particularly well suited for IRAs, Keoghs and other self-directed retirement plans.

One of these reasons concerns taxes, something that isn't a consideration in a tax-deferred account. Too many investment decisions are made because of the tax consequences attached to them. In a tax-deferred account, taking big gains when they appear presents no problem, as the holding period of six months and one day is of no consequence.

Too often, it's easy to rationalize why it makes sense to hold on for six months and a day and be taxed at the lower capital gains rate. But what an investor might have saved in taxes becomes almost academic: while waiting out the holding period, the stock has given back its gains and taxes are no longer a problem. The investor is left wondering why he didn't take his profits and glad to have had taxes to pay.

In tax-deferred vehicles, however, this type of logic doesn't come into play. Taxes are an issue only where losses are concerned and only then because losses in retirement programs are not deductible. In my own view, in some cases it may be suitable to regard these programs as tax-deferred trading vehicles that could prove to be almost obscenely profitable in a classic gold bull market. For those who can accept some risk with a portion of their retirement funds, I happen to think that self-directed programs are ideally suited for the volatility of the penny shares. Greater trading skills are required and it's not for everyone, but for those who can afford the risks, trading penny stocks is an overlooked strategy that many more investors should consider.

Penny Pitfalls

Having outlined some of the ways to help investors attain profits in penny mining shares, it's worth considering some of the common mistakes being made in hopes of avoiding them.

Overdiversification—Earlier I stressed the necessity

of owning a diversified portfolio of penny mining shares. Diversification spreads risks, thereby reducing them, and it also increases the odds of owning shares in a company whose shares skyrocket by 500 percent, 1,000 percent—or more. Nobody knows what's going to be found underground until a property is drilled, and having several irons in the fire enhances the possibility that drilling results on at least one of a company's programs will be positive.

While the merits of diversification are both logical and statistically irrefutable, my experience is that many investors carry this strategy to extremes—seemingly diversifying almost for the sake of it, not necessarily because it is the strategy that will generate the greatest profits. What these people often find is that their winners tend to get lost in the shuffle in a huge portfolio that's difficult to follow closely, unless, of course, one is making a full-time hobby of his investments.

Another side effect of being overdiversified is that it tends to make brokers rich (because small purchases exact much larger commissions), while virtually ensuring that investors never make a meaningful amount of money. Diversification is important, especially for new investors to this market, but it shouldn't preclude making serious money—not just the occasional big percentage gain that gets lost in the shuffle of a portfolio so large that it's almost impossible to follow anyway.

Own enough to make a difference—Investors never seem to own enough of their biggest winners, but they should own stocks in a disproportionate amount based on their experience in the market and on their expectations for individual stocks. The goal is to avoid being in the position of making huge gains in percentage points and only a negligible amount of money. Investors who really like a stock—and some are clearly more likeable than others—should also own more of it, not relegate it to a position of equality in a portfolio.

Just as diversification is more important for those who are inexperienced in these markets, buying according to expectations is something that is best done by those who have owned several penny shares and have gained some confidence in their judgment of these matters. Investors who feel their judgment can be trusted because they have the profits to show for it should also have more invested in stocks they feel best about. Gains of 1,000 percent and more can make for nice cocktail party chatter, but too often, these gains don't put children through college, pay off mortgages, buy houses at the beach, support favorite charities or pay for plane tickets to Europe. They can and, more often, they should.

Penny stocks **are** *speculative, but they* **are** **not** *gambling*—The risks of penny stocks have been well documented elsewhere in this book. As a group, these stocks are at the mercy of precious metals prices. Additionally, the minerals exploration business is dominated by failure, not success. In penny stocks, as in other speculative investments, it's important to accept the possibility that you will lose all that you invest. Investors who can't accept that proposition do not belong in such markets.

But, rather than just accepting the inherent risks of penny mining shares, it seems to me that too many investors are almost embracing these risks in a sense, investing in penny stocks and all but expecting to lose money. Such expectations may have been realistic during previous bull markets, but with gold currently selling for more than 1,200 percent above its old fixed price levels of $35 per ounce, gold mining today is an exceedingly profitable business.

Gold mining remains a speculative activity, but it is not the flagrant crapshoot it used to be. Barring a collapse of gold prices, choosing stocks with care and employing a contrary strategy to time purchases should produce profits much more often than losses. Appreciating the inherent risks of gold mining and expecting to make money most of the time is an attitude that predisposes investors toward making a profit. Equating investments in gold stocks to a day at the races or a trip to Las Vegas indicates an inaccurate perception of the current marketplace.

Conclusions

1. All of the advice in this book is contingent on the timing of its reading. To a large degree, the success or failure of any investment will be governed by the economic cycle and the timing of investments within it. Invest in the penny market according to your overall economic perspective, your degree of commitment to that perspective and your willingness and financial ability to accept the risks of gold mining.

2. Develop a strategy that suits your highly individual approach to the market. Diversify, buy when others are selling and sell when they are buying; have and employ a strategy for taking profits and avoid the mistakes most frequently made by others. At all costs, avoid the plight of those who buy the right stocks, ride them up in price and then fail to sell. Penny mining shares have been, and I believe will continue to be, a highly lucrative speculation—but only to those who isolate their profits. Never lose sight of the two main goals of investing: 1) generating profits and 2) realizing those profits. The current favorable environment for gold stocks is one that will not prevail for all time, but as this is written in August 1987, I think investors in gold stocks have only just begun to be rewarded.

5

"Most brokers don't know a mine from a pine cone."

Sam Parks

Brokers

Just as there are many possible choices for the investor in penny mining shares, there are even more brokers from whom one might make these purchases: full-service, full-price; discount brokers; specialized brokers, such as those who trade in penny mining stocks; U.S. and Canadian brokers; and even Canadian discount brokers. Even to market veterans, it sometimes seems as if finding a broker who suits your needs is no easier than finding a good stock. At least equal importance should be attached to the selection of each. But before an investor can find a broker from one of these categories who can fill his highly individual needs, the investor must first define what he's looking for.

First: Define Your Needs

There is not one correct answer to most people's questions about brokers. In some cases there may even be more than one answer. The answer(s) for each of you will depend on your investment goals, your level of investment knowledge, anticipated level of trading activity and your broker's ability to meet your individual needs. Before opening a new account with a client, all brokers require you to fill out forms to obtain basic financial information. One goal of this exercise is to establish the client's investment goals and define the parameters of the contemplated relationship. But before you can hope to tell a prospective broker what your goals are, you must first define them for yourself.

The most obvious distinction among investors is how they view the purchase of penny mining stocks. Some people regard penny shares as a cheap insurance policy with a big payoff in a time of high inflation. Most of this group have a buy-and-hold strategy; they don't follow prices or company developments closely, and they may well expect that a gold bull market will ultimately vindicate the losers in a portfolio. "When the wind blows, even the turkeys will fly" best describes the attitude and level of involvement these people choose to have with their penny portfolios. Obviously, this groups' needs for brokerage services are minimal, and the one-time or infrequent brokerage costs are of much less consequence to the overall success of most long-term investors' penny mining portfolios.

The active trader, on the other hand, has vastly different brokerage needs. To optimize buying and selling, a much closer working relationship is required between clients and brokers, and a high level of familiarity with how the penny markets work is presumed—not merely desired. The active investor is probably less likely to look to a broker for a steady stream of ideas and is instead looking for good execution of his orders. And because the level of activity in the account is higher, so should be the concern over the rate of commission. Like the so-called miracle of compound interest, frequent commissions can quickly run into serious money, especially if commissions are on the high end of the range.

Despite what I've just said, I think many investors are preoccupied with commissions when in fact they should be much more concerned with the skill of their broker in executing trades. People who are gleeful to think they saved a percentage point of commission on a purchase or sale of stock are often oblivious to sloppy brokerage practices that are almost invariably far more costly. The active trader needs to be more conscious of orders. The quality of brokerage service and stock recommendations is always more important than the cost of commissions.

In my view, whether an investor is oriented toward the long or short term is the key factor in determining the importance of commission to a penny portfolio. Other questions investors must answer before selecting a broker include:

1. Are you looking for advice or strictly execution? If you are looking for recommendations, how have the broker's previous picks fared for his clients? Is his basic strategy compatible with your own?

2. How does a broker communicate his recommendations to you? Does he phone, publish a client letter, tell you when to sell as well as when and what to buy?

3. Does he know anything about penny gold stocks or is he your "regular" broker, many of whom leave clients feeling that they're merely tolerating your desire to buy penny shares in hopes of cultivating more conventional brokerage business? Does he try to talk you out of a stock that you want to buy?

In the end, what you do with your broker's opinion is up to you. Unfortunately, trial and error is the only way to know when and whether a broker's input is valuable—or an unwanted distraction that sometimes prevents you from doing what you intended when you picked up the phone. If you want input, that's fine, but if a broker is forever asking "Why would you want to buy that?" you're dealing with the wrong broker. Finding the right broker is a highly individual quest and answering these questions—both before you look and during the audition period—will be instrumental to the success of the relationship. Defining the terms of the

broker/client relationship at the outset puts everyone involved in a better position to make a success of it.

Big Firms, Little Stocks

Many investors in penny mining shares choose to trade with
Big Board firms, usually because they already have an
account with one. "Convenience" is the sole criterion
applied, and matters of broker expertise and a willingness to
accept orders for penny gold shares rarely enter into the
choice. It is this group that Sam Parks, a former penny
broker himself, is talking about when he says "most brokers
don't know a mine from a pine cone." (In fairness to most
brokers, it could probably also be said that most penny gold
specialists don't know a cow chip from a computer chip.)

The Merrill Lynches, E.F. Huttons, Paine Webbers and
other mainstream firms don't need to know a mine from a
pine cone (if you're dealing with them, that's your job), but
they should at least be able to efficiently fill your order.
Sometimes this is possible, especially when NASDAQ-listed
stocks are involved or when you're buying a gold stock
that's listed in Toronto or on the American or New York
Stock exchanges. But often brokers with these major firms
don't even know how to pull up a quote on a Canadian
stock.

Not only do many of these brokers not know how to get
a quote on a Canadian stock, they're also not likely to be of
much help to you in figuring out currency conversions, to
say nothing of assessing the nuances of the market on an
individual stock. And they tend to come in with "market"
orders in illiquid markets. The net result is that the client
pays more. If they haven't a clue themselves what they're
doing, they're in no position to give you advice. Moreover,
as a general rule these people don't want your penny stock

business. It varies from firm to firm, but many of the large brokerage firms have rules prohibiting the purchase of stocks that sell for less than $5 or, even more commonly, those selling for less than $1. Not unlike getting a note from your doctor attesting to your presence of mind, many firms will require written permission from the branch manager before they'll place your order. Sometimes the regional manager's signature is required as well. Frequently, these brokers don't even make a commission on some of these trades; you can imagine how eager they are to conduct your penny stock business.

Aside from cumbersome internal policies and a general ineptitude regarding the purchase and sale of penny mining shares, another major problem with the big firms is their commission structure. Big firms have big commissions and this is especially true when penny stocks are being purchased. It's not uncommon to see commissions in the 10-12 percent range, and they often go higher. Sometimes a broker will come right out and tell you he doesn't want this kind of business, but if there were any doubt about it, ex-orbitant commissions are one indication that the firm prefers not to do business in penny stocks. The Big Board firms will take the business—but not without a stiff penalty.

There are exceptions to the stereotype I've painted of Big Board firms, but penny stocks are out of the mainstream and, in most cases, your broker should be as well. To me, paying full-service rates implies that you're receiving good service—not a disservice—and that your broker is worthy of his commission. If the stock ideas are yours, the commissions are high and your broker's familiarity with the market you choose to trade is nil, your continued use of that broker defies common sense. While full-service brokerages can work in the realm of penny stocks, too often big firms and little stocks just don't mix.

Special Brokers for Special Stocks

The shortcomings of Wall Street argue strongly in favor of specialists in the field of penny stocks. Many penny generalists are generalists in the sense that they often sell all varieties of penny shares, including mining stocks. If you're looking for ideas and feedback from a broker on penny mining issues, you're probably better off with someone who makes that area his exclusive province—or at least the majority of his business.

Mining stocks have always been an outgrowth of mining regions, and thus it should come as no surprise that the hotbeds of U.S. mining stocks are Denver, Spokane and Portland. Some brokers in these markets specialize in shares that trade in the local market, but most U.S. penny mining brokers are quite conversant with the Canadian markets; many of this group conduct the vast majority of their business in Canada. The reasons for doing business with a specialist are many: they know the companies, the markets and how they work, and their commissions aren't designed to turn business away. Not incidentally, they also want the business. Just as the importance of management cannot be overemphasized when choosing a stock, the difference between someone who knows what he's doing and someone who hasn't a clue can spell the difference between success and failure in the market. Don't let that outcome be determined by someone ill-equipped to meet your brokerage needs.

Many brokers unfamiliar with the Canadian markets grumble about "Vancouver bandits" when they think they've been taken advantage of, when in fact it's their own inexperience that produces this result.

Being ill-served in a buy-and-hold account may not prove too costly a mistake, but any degree of activity in an account will compound transaction losses associated with sloppy brokerage practices in a hurry. What clients don't know often *is* hurting them, and using "limit" orders is one elementary way of solving one of the most common problems of using a broker not conversant in the ways of the penny market. Another is to find a specialist.

Brokers: U.S. vs. Canadian

With most brokers not even in contention for your penny business, the issue is reduced to specialists on both sides of the border. There are definite advantages and disadvantages to each, and it really comes down to what suits the individual client's needs.

The biggest difference between Canadian brokers and their U.S. counterparts is this: commission. There are many other factors to consider, most of them more important than a few percentage points of commission, but in my experience it is the lower Canadian rates that are most often cited as the big advantage to doing penny resource stock business in Canada. This is especially true in an active trading account, where commissions often become a significant component of the account's overall performance.

In the United States, commissions start at around 5 percent for most penny brokers and work up to as much as 15 percent at some Wall Street firms; in Canada, the rates are much lower. The Vancouver Stock Exchange has a fixed rate of 3.3 percent (it used to be 3 percent, but a 10 percent surcharge was added several years ago); the Toronto, Montreal and Alberta markets all function under a negotiated commission structure. As such, these markets are often slightly more competitive. Alberta, which adopted negotiable commissions only recently, is generally regarded as less flexible on commissions than Toronto and Montreal. In all cases, and as in the United States, negotiable commissions depend on the size of the client, the order and the amount of time and research involved in filling the order.

Unlike in the United States where the SEC oversees all matters pertaining to securities, in Canada securities are a provincial matter, handled under the securities laws of the province and overseen by the various stock exchanges themselves. In the United States, brokerage firms are backed by SIPC; in Canada, a self-regulatory organization known as the Investment Dealer's Association has a safety net in place, the National Contingency Fund.

In addition to significantly lower commissions, one of the other advantages to doing business north of the border is the ability to purchase new issues of stock, but only under limited circumstances. Unless you're making private placements in Canadian companies at a prepublic stage, it is often difficult—if not impossible—to purchase Canadian stocks on an underwriting.

First, there is no residency requirement to purchase new issues in Canada. Of the $705.1 million (Canadian) raised by VSE-listed companies in 1986, 75.9 percent of this money was raised via private placements (9.6 percent of this amount came from U.S. investors). Much of this money was raised on a preprimary basis, that is, at a lower price than where the company begins trading when it comes to market. Such private placements are as close as the market comes to offering a "no-brainer." So-called seed stock that investors pay $.25 for and that subsequently begins trading at $.50, $1 and sometimes more is not a foolproof way to make money, but it's about as close as it gets.

One observer of the Canadian markets likens this company-birthing process to lighting a match. The people who hold the match first and pass it on have no problem, but the more hands it passes through, the greater the likelihood that someone is going to get burned. Getting in on the ground floor, usually under the auspices of a Canadian broker, is one way to avoid getting burned. In a normal stock distribution, starting in one of the Canadian markets and moving outward, the U.S. investing public is the likeliest recipient of the match in its waning moments.

Despite all the noise that's made about the advantages of buying new issues, in reality it's not a simple proposition even if you do have a Canadian account. First, you must have a broker with one or more hot deals in the pipeline and then you have to be a sufficiently good client to get a piece of the offering. Most people aren't going to be able to profit from this strategy and, ideally, they're better off being in at an earlier stage, such as a private placement, anyway.

Practically speaking, Canadian brokers can't sell new issues to U.S. citizens, simply because the securities cannot be sold outside the province, at least not on the initial underwriting. It would seem that it's the provincial angle that's responsible for the frequent misconception that only residents of the respective provinces can purchase new issues. In fact, it's the securities themselves that can't be sold outside the province.

One alternative to the provincial attitude toward new issues is to physically be in the province and solicit a new issue that you know is forthcoming. If you're in town, solicit an order *and* pay for it; it is possible to purchase new issues on the primary offering. In many instances you'll be required to sign a letter for the file stating that you were indeed in town and purchased the stock on an unsolicited basis.

Another way to purchase new issues in Canada is to form a Canadian company. This is a $50-and-a-boxtop-style gesture that will give you a lawful Canadian address. (Your company's address is usually that of a Canadian lawyer, who can form a company for $500-$600.)

Another one of the oft-cited disadvantages of doing business with U.S. brokers is their need to purchase shares in Vancouver—where most brokers will pay half the normal 3.3 percent commission—the net result being a double commission: Canadian commission is added to the standard U.S. rate. In reality, many of the specialists, precisely because they are active in the markets in these stocks, often match buyers and sellers in their own trading departments. In addition to off-exchange trading that goes on among clients in the back offices of U.S. brokerage houses that specialize in these markets, trading blocks of stock also goes on between firms. Many firms will cite this as an advantage and, if it is indeed one, it should be—and no doubt often is—reflected in a savings on commission.

Aside from avoiding the so-called "double commission," another real advantage is that the exchange of currencies is avoided, and thus another slight commission is saved. Perhaps a bigger advantage is the ability of a U.S. specialist in these stocks to make back-office markets, which can be a good deal for clients on both sides of the trade. For instance, let's say the market in a given stock is trading at $.55/$.65, with the last trade at $.65. In a case such as this, the difference would merely be split: the seller would receive $.60 for a stock the market is bidding at $.55; the buyer would receive a $.05 discount to what other buyers are paying at the same time.

Obviously, this technique won't work well for stocks with illiquid markets, but where it works, the specialist can accomplish this transaction to the benefit of both clients' accounts. Just try asking Merrill Lynch or one of the others to match up an order for Rockbottom Mines with a client on the other side of the trade.

While the lower commissions in Canada are definitely attractive, especially for the active trader, there are some drawbacks as well. One would certainly be the greater likelihood of winding up with a broker with a short-term perspective on the market, often referred to as a "flipper." In part because commissions are so low, the velocity of trading tends to be much faster in Canada, and this often works to the disadvantage of the client. Another drawback can be the logistics: brokerage firms can't afford to be at the mercy of the Canadian mails when dealing with U.S. clients, so in many instances they require U.S. investors to place funds in an account before investing any of it. Depositing money in advance—or big Federal Express bills—can be a logistical drawback, but if you find the right broker, that's a small inconvenience. If you find the wrong broker, you may wish you'd never heard of Canada.

Discount or Disservice?

The words above probably suggest that I don't have an open mind about discount brokers. I don't. My own experience with discount brokers leaves me admittedly biased, so perhaps the best place to begin is with my dealings with them. On several occasions, most recently in August 1986, I have attempted to purchase Canadian penny stocks in my wife's IRA account. She has an account with the giant of the industry, Charles Schwab, and they have internal policies that preclude buying and selling many Canadian stocks.

When I think of discount brokers I think first of Charles Schwab, but I also think of Technigen Platinum. As I was buying TGP for my own retirement account in August 1986, I phoned Schwab at the same time to enter a Technigen buy order in my wife's IRA account. As has happened on several previous occasions (high-flying Perron Gold among them), I was informed that Schwab could not purchase the stock. Schwab's policy is not to purchase Canadian stocks that are not also listed on an American stock exchange, on NASDAQ or in the "pink sheets" of over-the-counter stocks. That precludes a goodly percentage of Canadian stocks and almost always prevents an investor from buying new issues in the early aftermarket—as was the case with Technigen.

In my admittedly limited experience, this policy has meant huge opportunity costs: TGP was $1.50 when I bought it for my account and tried to purchase it for my wife's. The stock closed at $8 on January 30, 1987. That's a little better than 400 percent in five months, and also one reason I'm admittedly not very objective on the subject of discounters. Were those instances not reason enough, another reason that I'm not favorably disposed toward discount brokers is because phoning many of them is like phoning an airline. The line is busy or your call is placed on hold, seemingly forever. This phenomenon may become particularly pronounced as the Super Bull Market of 1982-87 inevitably begins to unravel.

In the end, my bias against discount brokers is that they seem to offer discounts on stocks I don't want to buy and—commission rates aside—have on several occasions prevented me from purchasing stocks that I did wish to own. Most specialists can save more by knowing what they're doing than you might possibly save through a discount broker. The Canadian stock exchanges all charge fees that approximate half of the "normal" rate, and U.S. discounters also must deal through a correspondent firm in Canada. My experience suggests that the opportunity costs are at least as meaningful as the fixed costs. Chalk up another one for the penny mining specialists.

Exceptions to my negative outlook on discounters would include the purchase of NASDAQ and other U.S.-listed stocks, where some savings could even be realized. My experience has shown this universe to be limited and the opportunity costs to be high. There are, however, some exceptions to my own experience, and even an alternative in Canada.

One alternative that some of you might wish to look into

is Marathon Brown, a Canadian discounter that will allow
you to employ margin and even short stocks, in both cases

Brokers: Types and Services

	Pros	Cons
Wall Street	Possibly convenience (you already have an account with one).	High commissions. Haven't a clue. Don't want the business. Don't know about penny stocks or mechanics of penny stock purchases.
U.S. Specialists	Knowledge level high.	Commission higher than Canadian. Don't buy at market (buy "right").
Canadian	Lower commissions. Good knowledge of gold stocks. Can purchase all Canadian stocks. Can purchase on margin. Can short the market. Offers international diversification. Different protection for investor.	Often difficult to find a good one. Due to mail and exchange rates, logistics can be a problem. Short-term perspective more prevalent. Different regulatory environment.
Discount	Can *sometimes* save money.	Often won't buy penny stocks. High minimum commissions and lack of market knowledge can preclude savings.

as long as they sell for more than $2. Marathon Brown's
Vancouver office indicated that stocks that sell for less than
$1.50 usually don't yield any savings. Furthermore, the
Vancouver and Alberta exchanges do not allow discounts on

trades, and on these Canadian exchanges discount brokers actually end up costing clients more. Like discount brokers everywhere, Canadian discounters are most advantageous to big clients. Like all Canadian accounts, 15 percent is withheld against interest and dividends (not applicable to most penny stocks), and a credit is allowed on your U.S. tax return. Also in the realm of taxes, it's worth mentioning that all foreign brokerage accounts in excess of $10,000 (U.S.) must be declared on line 11 of your Schedule B.

If you're interested in finding out more about Marathon Brown, their address is Suite 2010, 1040 W. Georgia St., Vancouver, B.C. V6E 4H2, 604-662-3707. I'm sure a Canadian discounter would prove more useful than any of the U.S. discount brokers with whom I've spoken.

Conclusions

1. Brokers can be largely responsible for your performance in the market, but ultimately each of you is responsible for the management of your investment funds. It's *your* money and *your* responsibility to see that your investment funds are in the hands of someone who is earning his commission, not merely collecting it.

2. The broker most likely to be deserving of a commission on a penny stock trade is the broker who specializes in the field. These people not only know how to perform the sometimes specialized transactions involved, they are also often excellent sources of new ideas and updates on old stories.

3. Even among specialists, brokers have their own areas of expertise and market philosophies. Be sure you've got a match before, not after, you begin to do business.

6

Picking Pennies

Just a few short years ago, there were two distinct schools of thought on the purchase of penny mining stocks. One was the random-walk approach, which maintained that the individual choice of stocks was much less important than being in the market when precious metals hysteria hits. This is the phase of the market that originally gave rise to the cliche "When the wind blows, even the turkeys will fly." Numerous studies have been performed—some of them so objectively random as to employ chimpanzees throwing darts—and many have bolstered the validity of the efficient market theory and the reliance that randomness places on *average* performances.

In the penny mining market, the father of the random walk is Norman Lamb, author of the classic *Small Fortunes in Penny Gold Stocks*. Norman's book was first published in 1973, and it drew heavily on his experiences during the unique boom in Spokane silver stocks from 1960 to 1968. On average, that market multiplied in value by a factor of 157, which is in itself an answer to the question "close your eyes or analyze?" Inasmuch as most of the stocks of that period defied conventional analysis anyway, it was hard to argue with the random approach.

In the late '70s and early '80s, perhaps the best-known

proponent of this method was best-selling author and advisor Doug Casey, who used to suggest choosing 20 stocks "whose first initials correspond to those of your mother's maiden name."

While that approach is arguably still a good one to take in the Spokane market, it's also important to note that I said Casey *used to* advocate this approach. Further, Norman Lamb himself doesn't choose stocks this way, simply because he knows how to distinguish real situations from those that only aspire to fly when all the turkeys take off. Aside from any specific expertise that Norman Lamb, Doug Casey or others could add to the selection process, the primary reason the random walk has lost favor in recent years is the altered economics of gold mining. While the discovery of a mineral deposit capable of attaining production is still a highly speculative proposition, gold exploration and development with gold selling at $450 (or even much less than that) is far more viable than it was at $35 gold.

The improved economics of gold mining have transformed the selection process from a blind crapshoot to a selective speculation; in short, to a market where the content of an investor's portfolio is far more important than the mere existence of it.

If the premise can be accepted that it *does* make a difference what a person owns, then it becomes important to understand that low-priced gold stocks (penny stocks) are not selected on the same basis as producing gold stocks. Whereas the evaluation of gold producers consists of weighing production costs, the potential for growth, price/earnings ratios, management and applying several yardsticks that help to isolate relative value, the selection of penny stocks is weighted heavily toward one factor: management.

Management

At the riskiest end of the penny stock spectrum, where an exploration company is the very definition of a crapshoot, investors are betting on the people behind the company. Certainly in the early stages of most junior mining companies, it would not be a misplacement of emphasis to say that the people behind the company *are* the company, or that this chapter could just as easily have been titled "Picking People." After management, every other consideration is secondary. To simplify even further, there are times when the only thing one needs to know is that certain people are behind a company; their involvement is easily the most important variable that additional research might reveal. It should be purchased, but the involvement of a Robert Friedland, a Dick Hughes, a Frank Lang or a Bruce McDonald—especially when they're on a hot streak—is often a reliable way to make money in the market.

To further this highly subjective analysis, just as knowing that certain people are involved can be the basis for an investment decision, it can also be the basis for a decision to avoid a purchase—or sell a stock short. I'm over-simplifying only slightly in saying that there are times when the story is almost superfluous and other times when "spare me the story" should be a knee-jerk reaction to the involvement of certain people. One of the first things investors need to understand about the junior mining business is that many of the people in it have absolutely no intention of making a mine. As my friend Jerry Pogue has often said, "They wouldn't know a mine if they fell into one." Such people are not looking to mine ore, but rather are exploring for a rich vein of investors who will drive up the price of their stock, sell into the buying they've created and then go on to the next one. One of the best ways to succeed in Vancouver is to prevent yourself from making mistakes in judging the people behind companies. This may sound cynical, but in Vancouver I happen to think it's only being realistic. "The richest mine can always be found in the purse of a fool" is an old saying of Vancouver stock promoters, and it's no less true there today than it was many years ago.

If the people are the most important variable in selecting a penny mining company, how does the investor arrive at conclusions about them? Contacts in the industry can help to discern a person's reputation; in some cases, people are preceded by their reputations. The way a person acquires a reputation is through his track record, which is generally a simple thing to get a handle on. What is the person's experience? Has he been associated with a producing mine in the past or, better yet, seen a property through from prospect to production? If so, is it still in production? Based on price alone, can it be termed a success story? How about a past affiliation with a major mining company? The latter isn't crucial (majors tend to be big, slow-moving dinosaurs whose styles are not always suited to small exploration/junior producing companies), but good working relationships with one or more majors can be a big plus.

A major's involvement also lends credibility, and news of a joint venture with a major is usually viewed positively by the market. No worthy project will go begging for a joint venture partner, but in a market where the object is to get into production to take the utmost advantage of the cyclical swings in gold's price, a running start toward this goal can only help.

It can be difficult to make judgments about management, but that is the first, and admittedly the most subjective, task investors are confronted with in the selection process. One of the places where investors are directly exposed to companies, and the people behind them, is at investment conferences and "dog and pony" shows where they're promoting their stocks. When you do see these people, do they seem to be more preoccupied with the market than with their project? Do you need sunglasses to cut the glare from the gold chains and pinky rings? Do you, at first glance, mistake the shrimp in their hospitality suite for lobster? In the final analysis, do you feel comfortable with the people and is there a basis for this comfort level? If not, buying the wrong people usually means that you've also bought the wrong stock.

Property

However talented a company's management may be, silk purses are not the product of sows' ears—nor are mines the result of moose pasture. The property is always *the* bottom line and a geologist's opinion is a starting point. If mines are such rare commodities, even a strong opinion from a geologist doesn't often bear fruit, but if the geologists aren't encouraged about a property, you shouldn't be either. Like management, geologists acquire reputations and build track records—good or bad—and it's important to know what this record shows. There are respected professionals and there are "armchair geologists" whose work is geared more toward public relations and higher stock prices than toward discovering mines. There's a greater concentration of geological expertise in Vancouver than anywhere else in the world, but there are also some geologists for hire who ask, "What kind of a report do you want me to write?" Assessing the merits of a property can sometimes be accomplished just by knowing whose name is on the geologist's report.

Aside from the level of geologic expertise at a company's disposal, another factor affecting a property is the location of the prospect. Mining is a game of odds, bad odds at that, but the odds of finding a discovery are enhanced if a company is at least exploring in a region where others have found gold.

This also applies to the examination of old producing properties, which gives rise to the adage to "look for a mine where there used to be one." At much higher precious metals prices, many old producers are going from being "mined out" to having substantial reserves—once again attaining production. Whether it's a raw prospect or an old mine, investing in companies whose claims are in areas of known mineralization is a more conservative approach than trying to forge new geological theories. Buying companies with multiproperty portfolios is another way to diffuse the risks associated with exploration. Multiproperty companies represent a many-irons-in-the-fire approach that enhances the probability of success, even if the success is only fleeting. Investors should be seeking opportunities for price appreciation; generally, the more available opportunities, the greater the likelihood that the investor will get a run for his money.

Capitalization

Capitalization, the number of shares outstanding multiplied by the current price of the stock, indicates what the marketplace believes a company is worth. A company with a low capitalization is generally preferred over one with a greater market value, simply because it has more inherent growth potential. Cheaper isn't always better, but in the hypothetical world where all things about two companies are equal, the cheaper stock is usually the one with the greater potential. A higher price or market value can be a sign that a stock is overvalued or, like Xerox since its penny-stock days (when it was named American Haloid), it's already achieved a degree of respectability—and the biggest gains are behind it. The idea is to buy cheap in *anticipation* of a respectability that will be accompanied by higher prices. Stocks with low capitalization simply have more growing room left in them.

Five million shares outstanding would generally be preferable to 20 million shares, because new buying will have a greater impact on the price of the stock. For example, a single investor—on his own—could double or triple the price of many penny stocks (and these stocks would likely return to their former levels when this individual stopped buying). Virtually any investor could buy IBM stock all day long, every day, and it wouldn't affect the price of the stock.

The "float" in a stock is the number of shares that trade freely in the market; generally, the more closely held the stock is, the more volatile. The less stock available to the market, the greater the price swings will be in response to new buying. A key component of a stock's float is the number of shares held by insiders: company officers, directors and others who have significant holdings, usually acquired at prices substantially below the prevailing market price. The amount of stock held by insiders is an indication of management's incentive to perform. In those cases where management is involved with several companies, identifying where management's self-interest lies is often a good way to determine which of their stocks to buy. There are a number of excellent management groups in Vancouver with many companies under their stewardship, but only a fraction of them are worth owning at any given time. Buying the "right people" isn't enough; good management must be focusing their attention on a company to justify its ownership.

Insider stock, and management's attitude toward it, can often give clues to the future management foresees for the company. In Canada and the United States, insider stock is "restricted." In Canada such stock can be sold in increments of 25 percent of the total position every 90 days; in the States, SEC Rule 144 requires a two-year hold, after which the stock can be sold off in stages. Insider selling can mean anything from having to raise funds to send a child to college, to prudent profit taking, to blowing out of a position while the market is up and the company's prospects are grim (unknown to the general market). Some people have a history of being involved with companies for speculative purposes rather than business purposes, a phenomenon that's much more common in Canada. But without an established history of management's activity in the market, quizzing management on their intentions sometimes yields the desired information. The timing of insider selling can be especially important, because when restricted stock hits the market, it tends to do so in large blocks and frequently depresses the price. Knowing that such selling is on the way can help investors time their purchases.

Dilution

In mining, one meaning of "dilution" is waste rock that is removed along with ore in the mining process. Another, and often more important meaning, is the extent to which a company's capitalization is affected by warrants and options that may be outstanding but not yet exercised. The term "fully diluted" describes the number of shares in existence once all options and warrants have been exercised. Prior to that, they are not included in the number of shares outstanding.

The effects of dilution are twofold:

• It adversely affects potential earnings per share, because the earnings must be apportioned among a greater number of shares. It would be like Joe DiMaggio using one bat throughout his 56-game hitting streak or alternating among a half dozen. As a collector's item, the one bat would be worth much more, just as earnings split among fewer shares are worth more than when divided among a larger number.

• When options or warrants are exercised, the amount of stock available to the market grows, usually causing a short-term price decline, or exacerbating one already in progress. The market frequently requires time to digest an influx of new stock. Short term, dilution has a great deal to do with the way a stock will trade. Long term, dilution affects earnings potential, something which is a moot point in many exploration plays anyway.

Promotion/Market Visibility

Promotion and market visibility are related factors that can have a great effect on a stock's ability to rise in price. Though most investors don't care why the price of their stock is rising, they're better off if the price rises on fundamentals, not hype that will inevitably run its course. The long-term investor needs to make greater efforts to distinguish between "real deals" and stock distribution schemes. Those who dabble in short-term stock plays need to know the difference so they don't overstay their welcome in a stock that may rise fast and perhaps fall even faster.

Buying into an obvious stock promotion and relying on the "greater fool" theory is not a recommended strategy, but if you adopt it, just be sure you're buying—and selling—early. For instance, if you notice a number of advisory services and brokers recommending the same stock all at once, it's the closest thing to a foregone conclusion that the stock will rise in price. But when new buying is exhausted and a number of advisory services are already on the bandwagon, there's no one left to fuel new interest in the stock. Predictably, such stocks decline in price—hopefully, after you've already sold.

Promotion is a word fraught with bad connotations when referring to a stock. In Canada, promoters come in all varieties, some of them justly deserving of the bad images the word conjures up. Others are just businessmen trying to run their companies the best way they know how. To distinguish between the two and arrive at an admittedly subjective conclusion, an investor needs to ask himself some questions: Do the people involved seem preoccupied with the price of the stock, often going so far as to make predictions about the price and the time it will require to get there? Do they have a track record in exploration or mining or do they seem to be just mining the public? Are they spending inordinate sums of money on flashy reports, a blizzard of press releases from PR firms and broker excursions and reaching for $500 dinner checks at the same time they're giving lip service to "putting the money into the ground"?

Often, there's more gold and silver in the names of these companies than they will ever find in the ground, and some of the indicators listed above should serve as red flags to keep you from letting your investment dollars succumb to a promotion. Whereas promotion describes the efforts of a company to make its story known to the investment community, another aspect of market visibility is a function of the market(s) a stock trades in. Because most Canadian companies trade on exchanges in Vancouver or Toronto, this distinction applies chiefly to U.S. companies, which trade either over the counter or on NASDAQ.

OTC stocks are quoted each day in the National Quotation Bureau's "pink sheets." Trading in them takes place on the telephone, one trading desk buying from the market maker with the best price (traders are required to check among three, assuming there are that many). Many of the stocks listed in the "pinks" trade inactively, and following prices closely (unnecessary in any case) requires you to become a broker's pest or subscribe to one of the many services that supply quotes. The mere fact that many issues are inactive, the difficulties encountered in following them and frequent disparities in price among market makers argues for having especially good reasons to purchase non-NASDAQ, OTC stocks.

Although many times a stock's greatest appreciation occurs prior to gaining a NASDAQ listing, the advantages of a broader listing usually outweigh the drawbacks listed above. One advantage is that NASDAQ-listed stocks can be obtained by any broker merely by punching the symbol into the quote machine on his desk, after which a representative bid and ask price appear on his screen. If you want to follow your purchases closely, a NASDAQ listing makes this easy.

Because many people purchase only those stocks whose prices they can check in the morning paper, a NASDAQ stock's relatively high profile encourages new buying and, because at least three market makers are required to attain a listing, NASDAQ stocks generally have better liquidity. It also indicates that a company has passed some financial hurdles that favor investors' getting a better run for their money. That, after all, is what is being sought.

Crunching the Numbers

All that's been discussed thus far pertains mostly to exploration plays and, to a lesser degree, development companies and junior producers. Compared with the research that's applied to seasoned companies with assets and earnings, analyzing most exploration plays is a matter of flying by the seat of your pants. But once a company has spent enough money drilling holes, it slowly acquires the data that's necessary to justify taking the property into production, shelving it while awaiting higher prices—or abandoning it rather than throwing good money after bad.

To make these judgments, the key variables a company must possess are these: tonnage (size of ore body/blocked out reserves), costs (to mine and mill the ore), grade (ounces per ton) and recovery (percentage of metal recovered from processing). Combined, these factors determine whether a project is economic and form the basis for calculating future earnings potential.

The following example outlines the steps required to reach a decision on production and estimates what the company's stock should be selling for. The numbers are real—only the name of the company has been changed. In this real case with a hypothetical name, four years of drilling and $18 million were required to obtain these numbers.

Estimated Earnings Per Share Computations

Company: Fool's Gold, Inc.
Estimated grade of ore: .065 ounces per ton
Estimated recovery: 85 percent
Estimated production: 10,000 tons per day
Estimated mine/mill costs: $12 per ton
Estimated production days: 350 per year
Company's working interest: 50 percent

The *grade of ore* is obtained by performing thousands of assays on drill core samples. A few drill holes may be indicative of future drill holes, but unless a property has been subjected to an extensive drilling program, spectacular results in a small sampling of drill holes is meaningless.

Mineral recovery from the ore is a metallurgical and milling problem. Sometimes the metallurgy is complex and requires special processes to separate the metal from the host rock. Laboratory testing and small-scale "pilot plant" operations answer these questions for the company. The goal is to obtain an optimum recovery, i.e., the highest recovery for the lowest possible cost.

Estimated production is a function of the reserves that

have been blocked out by drilling. The size of the ore body determines whether a company spends $20 million or $200 million to mill the ore and it also has a bearing on the life of the mine. A combination of variables is considered to yield the optimum amount of gold for the lowest commitment of capital.

Estimated mine and mill costs can be calculated once the optimum processing facility has been designed.

Estimated production days are just that: the number of days a project can be worked. Whether the operation is underground or open-pit, and the weather in places as diverse as Alaska and Arizona, Canada and California, dictate the number of days per year that a mine can operate.

In this example, the *working interest* is 50 percent. This means that the company has a joint venture partner and must earn its share by spending 50 percent of the costs of exploration and development. If the company had a "carried interest," this would mean that the company would get a "free ride" for bringing the property to the major. The major company then puts up all the money to earn a shared interest in the property.

As everything hinges on the validity of these numbers, it's also important to know where they come from. Major mining companies who produce such numbers can usually be assumed to be credible, as can outside engineering firms who are often called in to perform feasibility studies. But if a small company has produced an average grade, recovery percentage and the other crucial numbers entirely on its own, the numbers cannot be assumed to be accurate. Outside verification is crucial. Too many small companies, especially Canadian ones, drill a dozen holes and start extrapolating. This method may produce a nice stock play, but it generally doesn't result in mines.

Once solid numbers are in hand, which in this case took four years and $18 million, the economic merit of a project can be determined and rough earnings calculations can be estimated. Assuming the grade, recovery and costs remain relatively constant, the biggest variable is the price of gold.

Because this particular project will require $250 million to put into production, the time value of money is a major factor. Contrary to appearances that this project would be profitable at $300 gold, Fool's Gold, Inc., would actually require $400 gold to make money. And, the higher gold rises above $400, the more money it would make.

Fool's Gold, Inc.
Estimated Earnings Per Share

		At Gold Price of			
		$300	**$500**	**$800**	**$1,000**
Est. grade of ore: oz./ton		.065	.065	.065	.065
Est. recovery: 85 percent	x	.85	.85	.85	.85
Net grade/ton		.055	.055	.055	.055
Price of gold	x	300.00	500.00	800.00	1,000.00
Gross profit per ton		16.50	27.50	44.00	55.00
Less est. mine/mill cost	−	12.00	12.00	12.00	12.00
Net profit per ton		4.50	15.50	32.00	43.00
Est. production: tons/day	x	10,000	10,000	10,000	10,000
Net profit per day		45,000	155,000	320,000	430,000
Est. production days	x	350	350	350	350
Total net profit (in millions)		15.75	54.25	112.00	150.50
Co. percent working interest	x	50%	50%	50%	50%
Net profit to company (in millions)		7.875	27.125	56.000	75.250
No. shares outstanding (fully diluted, in millions)	÷	4.55	4.55	4.55	4.55
Est. earnings per share		$1.73	$5.96	$12.31	$16.54

Leverage is sometimes a difficult concept to grasp as it pertains to mining operations, but the table makes the point dramatically: as the price of gold rises from $300 to $500, a 66 percent increase, projected earnings rise by 244 percent.

At $800 gold, a 166 percent increase from $300, the earnings jump by 711 percent. The current price of gold and, sometimes more importantly, the market's expectations for gold are the variables that will make or break a project—and justify much higher prices for a company's shares.

Conclusions

1. In the penny mining markets, it does make a difference what investors purchase. Those who suggest otherwise in the current environment are either rationalizing a lazy approach to the market or are oblivious to the enhanced economics of gold mining and the greater availability of information to investors.

2. The people behind a company are the most important factor to consider, followed by property (or properties), capitalization and promotional considerations. The sum total of these variables should answer the question "What is it about this stock that's going to make it rise in price?"

7

*"When a man owns mines but is
ignorant of the art of mining,
then it is advisable that he
should share in common with
others the expenses not of one
only, but of several mines."*

**Georgius Agricola,
De Re Metallica, 1556**

Gold Stock
Mutual Funds

As an advocate of penny stocks, I've always viewed gold
funds primarily as a tool of diversification. While the funds
have a history of doing well in gold bull markets, I've always thought it important that people not expect penny-
stock-style performance from a fund. That's still true, but
the performance of the gold funds in 1987 requires no
apologies. The creation of new funds, the prospect of higher
gold prices and the limited supply of stocks available helps
explain the remarkable performance of some gold stocks in
1987—and will be a major factor in determining the still
higher prices of tomorrow.

The historical performance of all mutual funds suggests
that success begets failure and that last quarter's big winner
is often this quarter's big loser. The volatility and cyclical
nature of the precious metals has made the success/failure

syndrome particularly pronounced in the gold-oriented funds, a phenomenon that was most recently evident in the first and second quarters of 1987. In the first quarter, gold-oriented mutual funds occupied eight of the top 10 spots among the 1,278 mutual funds monitored by Lipper Analytical Services. In the second quarter, there were no gold funds in the top 10; one had to look to the 20th spot (Shearson Lehman) to find the top performing gold fund. There were no others among the top 50 funds.

As proxies for gold stocks, the gold-oriented mutual funds have an enviable long-term record—in spite of the often hot and cold appearance of their short-term performances. According to Lipper, gold-oriented funds averaged 759 percent over the 10-year period ending June 30, 1987, easily outpacing the Dow Jones Industrial Average (347 percent) and the mutual fund industry average (376 percent). And despite the up and down nature of the gold funds during the first two quarters of 1987, as a group the gold funds have logged an impressive performance during the year.

Mutual funds that invest primarily in gold stocks are a growing force in today's gold equity markets and are likely to play a much greater role in the current bull market than they have in the past. In 1979, the eight U.S. gold-oriented mutual funds had assets totaling less than $200 million. At the beginning of 1987, the 24 U.S. gold funds had combined assets of $2.2 billion. Thanks to higher gold prices, higher stock prices and new money, the assets of these same 24 funds now total more than $5 billion. In the past eight years, the number of funds has tripled and the value of the funds has multiplied 25 times over—much of this growth occurring during a period of generally declining prices, at that.

The growth of the gold funds is nothing short of spectacular; many of the funds have doubled and tripled their assets in a matter of months. International Investors, the oldest and largest gold fund, took in $108 million in April 1987 alone, against $109 million during all of 1986. In the context of a lowly 15 percent move in gold, it doesn't require much imagination to conclude that the funds will have a huge impact on gold stock prices as the precious metals markets enter a more dynamic phase. But these increases, both in percentage terms and in dollar amounts, are just in the U.S. gold funds. This overlooks the huge pools of capital in Europe seeking refuge in North American gold stocks. In the heartland of gold stocks, Canada witnessed the creation of four gold funds in 1983 and several in-house funds have since been launched by Canadian brokerage firms. Nomura Securities, the giant Japanese securities firm, has a fund in registration and several other funds are in the process of becoming available to the public. The term "self-fulfilling prophecy" is often used to describe an influx of buying in penny shares, and the inflow of capital from gold funds is likely to have a similar self-fulfilling effect on the entire universe of gold stocks before this cycle has run its course.

Aside from the enviable long-term track record of the gold funds, one of the primary reasons for their mushrooming growth is a fundamental change in the way gold is viewed. Just a decade ago gold was an exotic (many would say kooky) speculation. In the realm of modern portfolio management, however, gold has made the transition from wild-eyed speculation to an insurance policy no prudent man or woman should be without. Prior to 1979, portfolio managers were bound by risk tests applied to each component within a portfolio. Today's "prudent man" test of risk is applied to total portfolio risk. Under this revision of portfolio theory, gold serves as a hedge against the risks of investment assumptions being wrong elsewhere in the portfolio. In short, gold has been embraced as a hedging tool and a necessary component of any well-diversified portfolio.

In the future, I believe that the increased investment demand of the new funds will be one of the reasons gold stocks will attain unprecedented heights in the bull market that is only now beginning to enter the dynamic phase. The same phenomenon that drove the stock market—too much money with no place to go—will come to bear on the gold stocks. If the flow of funds earlier in 1987 is any indication, the single biggest contribution to this mania is likely to come from the gold funds. Recent events on Wall Street also lead me to conclude that the fund route is how many of tomorrow's investors will choose to play the gold market.

Gold Funds: Pros and Cons

Like conventional mutual funds, gold funds offer advantages and disadvantages over direct investment in the share market. For both large and small investors, mutual funds offer a degree of diversification not readily available in individual portfolios. and the buyer of mutual fund shares is receiving professional management of the portfolio. In theory, and sometimes in practice, this means superior results, but it always means that the investor doesn't have to make any decisions beyond which fund to purchase. The fund manager does all the buying and selling. The share buyer is either a hero or goat, depending on his choice of fund and timing of its purchase.

Although there are currently 24 U.S.-based funds that invest in bullion and precious metals equities, not all of these so-called gold funds are interchangeable with one another. Some invest primarily in South African gold stocks, while the charters of others specifically forbid South African investments; some funds have high bullion components, others confine their holdings to equities; some funds have commission charges or "loads," many others are no-load funds.

Most of today's funds enjoy the ease of access of toll-free numbers, telephone switch privileges and a variety of alternatives to keep investors' money in the "family" when their sector of choice begins to look unattractive. The differences among the funds are often profound and are best perceived before—not after—you invest your money in one of them.

The Canadian Funds

Despite Canada's long history of gold production, gold-oriented funds were few and relatively small in comparison to the proliferation of U.S. gold funds. The remarkable performance of the U.S. funds during the 1979-80 bull market did not go unnoticed by the Canadians, however. Goldcorp was the first of four new Canadian closed-end funds. Offered in May 1983, Goldcorp had hopes of raising $40 million (Canadian). Instead, $175 million was raised in six weeks. Although the fund was designed to appeal to the institutional investor, approximately $115 million of the total came from individuals, approximately half from the Far East. The discovery of this unknown demand among individual investors was not lost on others: three new funds immediately began to organize public offerings.

Within six months, the funds had raised $404 million, which represented 10 percent of all the equity capital raised in Canada in 1983. Some of the success of the funds can be attributed to the fact that, for the first time, insurance companies, pension funds and various retirement programs had a vehicle through which to acquire exposure to gold bullion and, more importantly, to mining equities, many of which were regarded as too small for institutional investors.

Unlike the majority of the U.S.-based gold mutual funds, which sell an unlimited number of shares, all four of the Canadian funds are closed-end investment corporations. The closed-end fund is so named because the number of outstanding shares is limited. ASA, the South African fund, is undoubtedly the best known closed-end fund. Shares in closed-end funds trade on a securities exchange (New York in the case of ASA; Toronto for the four Canadian funds) or in the OTC market. Again, unlike most open-end mutual funds, buyers and sellers deal with one another through the medium of the stock exchange, not with the fund itself. As with other stocks, the price of a closed-end fund's shares is determined by supply and demand and prevailing market conditions. The buyer of a closed-end fund is buying professional management and the asset mix of the fund.

There are times when shares in a closed-end fund trade at a premium to the net asset value of the fund. At other times, shares sell at a discount to net asset value. (Net asset value is the market value of the fund's investments, minus any liabilities.) It reflects greater demand for the individual fund than for the sum demand of its components (the stocks themselves) when funds trade at a premium. ASA, for example, has a history of trading at a premium, a condition caused by more people wanting to purchase ASA than wanting to purchase the individual shares in ASA's portfolio. Convenience and ease of access to a specific sector of the market help account for this condition.

Open-end funds, like all of the U.S. gold-oriented funds, have no limit to the number of shares they can sell. Such funds are continually issuing new shares as purchases are made and redeeming shares when shareholders wish to sell. And unlike the closed-end funds, which manage a fixed amount of money raised on the initial offering, the open-end funds receive the largest infusions of cash when it is most disadvantageous to invest. Money tends to come at market tops and leave at market bottoms, precisely the opposite of what a fund manager would prefer.

There is always a publicly traded market for closed-end shares, where individuals sell to one another on a stock exchange. In contrast, the open-end fund must always be prepared to redeem shares at their net asset value. This can be disadvantageous to the fund in volatile markets, but it can also be a strong plus to a new purchaser. Three of the best known Canadian gold funds—Goldcorp, BGR Precious Metals and MVP—all currently trade at discounts. There are several reasons for the traditional discount to the net asset value of the Canadian funds:

1. Tradition—things tend to emulate their history, and the history, so far, of Canadian funds is that they trade at discounts.

2. Shareholders lack direct control in the management of the funds and this has a tendency to be reflected in the price of the funds' shares.

3. The number of funds dilutes the interest that would otherwise be focused on one or two funds. This explains the premiums currently enjoyed by ASA and Central Fund and the much larger premiums—in excess of 100 percent—built into the Korea and Taiwan funds.

4. Canadian funds are taxed at the fund level as well as at the shareholder level (when sold) and the tax on unrealized gains is factored into the net asset value of the funds.

In the brief reviews of the Canadian funds that follow, the stock symbol for each of the funds follows its name. All trade on the Toronto Stock Exchange. Goldcorp and BGR Precious Metals also trade in Montreal; Central Fund also trades on the American Stock Exchange (AMEX). The net asset value of shares in each fund is calculated at the close of business each Thursday and is published each Saturday in the *Globe and Mail*'s "Report on Business" section.

Goldcorp (T:G)

Goldcorp was the first of the Canadian funds and, at $220 million (Canadian), remains the largest. The fund's investment policy requires that at all times at least 75 percent of the market value of Goldcorp's noncash assets be invested in gold-related investments. The portfolio's current mix is 52 percent gold bullion, 26 percent Canadian mining stocks, 15 percent South African shares, 5 percent U.S. and Australian mining equities; 2 percent is in cash and other assets.

Of the four funds, the historical price swings have made Goldcorp the best trading vehicle. It is also the only one of the Canadian funds that can be followed daily in *The Wall Street Journal.*

(Goldcorp Investments Ltd., P.O. Box 68, IBM Tower, T–D Centre, Toronto, ON M5K 1E7, 416-865-0326.)

Central Fund (T:CEF.A), (AMEX:CEF)

The articles of Central Fund of Canada Ltd. require that not less than 85 percent of the noncash assets of the fund be invested in gold and silver bullion in bar form. Gold and silver bullion currently make up 91.6 percent of Central Fund's $110 million in net assets (93,188 ounces of gold, 4.4 million ounces of silver). Central Fund is the purest hard asset fund, and this high bullion component is also the reason that it's the only one of the closed-end funds to ever trade at a premium to net asset value.

In April 1987, when people were clamoring to gain exposure to bullion, many investors were opting for Central

Fund in their IRAs and RRSPs (the Canadian equivalent of an IRA) and the demand for the fixed number of shares in the fund resulted in a brief premium of 21 percent. In line with a pullback in bullion, Central Fund settled back to a premium of 2-4 percent above net asset value. It's become clear that Central Fund is being perceived as the vehicle of choice by investors unwilling to accept the risks and high valuations currently placed on gold stocks but still seeking legal exposure to bullion. Market analyst Ian McAvity is a director and advisor to Central Fund.

(Central Fund of Canada Ltd., P.O. Box 7319, Ancaster, ON L9G 3N6, 416-648-7878.)

BGR Precious Metals (T:BPT.A)

BGR is an acronym for Beutel Goodman Rothschild; Beutel Goodman & Co. Ltd. of Toronto is the fund's advisor on North American precious metals equities; N.M. Rothschild Asset Management Ltd. of London manages non-North American precious metals equities; Guardian Trustco International of Toronto is the advisor on BGR's investments in bullion. BGR's current portfolio contains 20 percent in gold and silver bullion, 45 percent in North American shares, 10 percent in South Africa, 15 percent in Australia and 10 percent in cash. The BGR portfolio management team includes Peter Cavelti and Pierre Lassonde, and their active management of the fund produced the best track record of the Canadian funds during 1986. BGR was up 57 percent in 1986 and the fund again outperformed the competition in the first half of 1987, up 41.7 percent through July 24.

(BGR Precious Metals Inc., c/o Montreal Trust Co., 15 King St. W., Toronto, ON M5H 1B4, 416-363-5621.)

Guardian-Morton Shulman (T:GMS)

Guardian-Morton Shulman was the brainchild of author/ physician/investment advisor Morton Shulman. Although conceived in the spirit of a gold-stock fund, GMS has been in a cash position throughout much of its existence. Employing a trend-following trading system, the portfolio manager traded gold for much of 1986 and 1987, without much success. The fund currently has 92 percent of its $45 million portfolio invested in gold bullion and certificates. But, in view of the fund's erratic track record and its earlier departure from its stated purpose, I don't think Guardian-Morton Shulman is worthy of consideration as a gold fund. If you own shares in it, you should be looking to own something else.

Prospector Fund (Open End)
New Prospector Fund (Open End)

In response to a growing market for gold shares and a specific desire to appeal to the investor seeking alternatives to South African gold stocks, the United Services family unveiled the Prospector Fund in August 1983. United Services is one of the largest gold funds and its South African portfolio has one of the best long-term track records in the business, up 816 percent over the 10-year period ended June 30, 1987.

Prospector's charter prevented it from purchasing South African shares; thus, the emphasis has been on North American and Australian precious metals companies, with the occasional resource company included as well. In the interest of liquidity, the core of the portfolio is made up of senior gold and silver producers (40-45 percent), while the remainder of the fund is invested in junior producers (30-35 percent) and, to a much lesser degree (approximately 15 percent), developmental and exploration companies.

Based on the advisor's track record with the gold fund, and also because Prospector was clearly in the right place at the right time—selling a North American-only gold fund when the shift was most pronounced away from South Africa—the concept was a popular one. Unfortunately, in 1985 it became apparent that the concept, however good, was being poorly executed. That has since changed, but the history of Prospector is worth a review.

After recommending Prospector on more than one occasion in *Penny Mining Stock Report*, it later became glaringly apparent that Prospector's performance was seriously lacking. It also came to my attention that there were grave problems with some of the holdings in the fund's portfolio and the rumor mill was also active.

As a result of his activity, the fund was in multiple violation of Investment Company Act guidelines: Prospector had purchased more than 10 percent of the voting securities of any one issuer; invested more than 5 percent of its assets in securities of companies with less than three years of continuous operation; and invested more than 5 percent of its assets in securities of any one issuer. As a result of these violations, the SEC refused to renew the fund's prospectus. Thus, the fund was not allowed to take in new investments and could only make redemptions to existing shareholders.

While the problems of the original Prospector fund were in the process of being sorted out, the fund's advisor began taking in new investments under a new prospectus. This accounts for the two versions of Prospector today, one known as Prospector (the original, still open only to redemptions), the other known as New Prospector. Like the original, New Prospector purchases resource stocks anywhere in the world outside of South Africa. The current mix of the portfolio is approximately 25 percent in Australian mining stocks, 45 percent in Canadian companies, 20 percent in U.S. companies and 10 percent in cash.

In the first quarter of 1987, United Services Advisors, the funds' manager, had three of the top 10 performing funds among the 1,278 monitored by Lipper Analytical Services—including both versions of Prospector. New Prospector began trading at $1 on November 22, 1985. On April 18, 1987, the fund peaked at $2.61.

The litigation surrounding this entire episode is still being sorted out, but much of the loss sustained by the previous portfolio manager has been reclaimed. The current portfolio manager is someone I encounter in my travels; in addition to being an extremely nice fellow with solid geological credentials, he has an excellent track record in almost two years on the job. Prospector Fund appears to me to be back on track. If Prospector's aggressive portfolio suits your needs, I would once again feel comfortable with funds under their management.

(Prospector Fund, c/o United Services Advisors, Inc., P.O. Box 29467, San Antonio, TX 78229, 800-531-5777.)

MVP Capital Corp. (T:MVP)

MVP, the creation of well-known Canadian advisor Ian McAvity, is a Toronto-based closed-end gold fund with some key differences that distinguish it from the competition. Modeled on the mining finance houses of Europe, MVP is essentially a holding company for stock in companies that have issued flow-through shares. With the flow-through tax advantages for Canadian investors drawing to a close, MVP appears well positioned to profit from an active role as a mining finance house. MVP has targeted small- to medium-sized Canadian development companies and currently holds positions in 41 of them (including several recommended in Appendix I).

MVP's Exploration Advisory Committee is at least equally impressive: geologist David Bell, a member of the team credited with the Hemlo discovery; Peter Ferderber, one of Canada's best-known and most successful prospectors; Terence Flanagan, president of Muscocho and vice president of Flanagan McAdam; John Hansuld, president of Canamax Resources and Bruneau Mining; and Malcolm Taschereau, former president of Dome Mines and Campbell Red Lake.

Unlike most gold funds, which diversify across the spectrum, MVP concentrates its investments in the low-priced end of the market and looks more like a penny mining closed-end mutual fund than any of the others. The idea behind the MVP Fund was to locate a source of financing for companies that progress beyond the exploration stage, at which point MVP would step in to raise the financing for the development and production phases. Through a public offering in December 1986, MVP raised $43.5 million in equity and flow-through partnerships, which funded more than $36 million in precious metals exploration programs in the 1986-87 winter drilling season. As of July 15, 1987, MVP had raised $70 million of a target of $85 million in flow-through partnerships, which will be taken over by MVP in April 1988. This will put MVP's asset base over $100 million at today's prices and will raise its ownership to 10-20 percent in more than a dozen evolving gold producers.

The money raised for the flow-through partnerships is rolled into a holding company, for which shares in MVP Capital are exchanged on a share-for-share basis. Stripping away the complexities of the original investment and the tax ramifications, investors who purchase shares in MVP own shares in a portfolio of excellent emerging companies. As in the case of the other Canadian closed-end funds, MVP shares trade *at a discount* to the net asset value of the fund. MVP shares on the Toronto Stock Exchange recently traded at a 23 percent discount to estimated net asset value. In a good gold market, I expect the shares will not only be up substantially, but will also be selling at a premium to net asset value.

For the person seeking diversification and a more conservative way to own penny stocks, MVP is a solid choice that should more closely resemble a "penny" fund than any of the other open-end and closed-end gold funds.

(MVP Capital Corp., 20 Richmond St. East, Suite 425, Toronto, ON M5C 2R9, 416-867-1100.)

Conclusions

1. Investors have many alternatives available through gold stock funds. Given investors' recent history of playing the stock market via the fund route, the many varieties of funds will be a growing force in the developing market for gold shares. While I still don't think gold funds should be considered the equivalent of owning individual penny mining stocks, the advantages of diversification, professional management, low transaction charges, switch privileges and all the other trappings people got used to during the extended boom in Wall Street stocks will be an explosive combination during a classic bull market in gold. Among the Canadian closed-end funds, professional management and ease of access to a diversified portfolio will in all likelihood result in significant premiums to net asset value.

2. The performance of gold stocks in the first quarter of 1987 occurred during a period of relatively stable gold prices, once again displaying gold's tendency to move *after* the stocks. What's important to remember is that this took place during a period when inflation was low (albeit rising) and the overall investment climate did not favor the purchase of gold-related assets. What will happen when the financial environment *does* favor gold stocks?

3. My instinctive preference is for the Canadian funds, specifically BGR and MVP. They trade at discounts, are not subject to the cycle of cash infusions and redemptions and are dependent on the fund manager's abilities. Among U.S. funds, my leaning would be toward New Prospector. The composition of the portfolio, my familiarity with management and the fund's recent track record make this an easy choice.

My preferences may not square with your own, but if you can't find a gold fund that suits your needs, it's only because you haven't figured out what you're looking for. As in the realm of individual gold stocks, there's something for everyone in the universe of gold funds.

8

*"The rule on staying alive
as a forecaster is to give
'em a number or give 'em
a date, but never give
'em both at once."*

Jane Bryant Quinn

Where We're Going

Mrs. Quinn's advice is solid and I'll not violate it at this late stage of the book. Although I have a strongly held opinion on the subject, I don't *know* where the gold market is headed, nor do I have any particular insight into the length of time it will take to arrive at its next cyclical peak. Contrary to a great number of projections and much guesswork on behalf of this elusive number—and the time frame within which it will occur—I don't think anyone else has the answers to these questions either.

Flying in the face of Mrs. Quinn's counsel, my own guess is that gold will easily exceed its 1980 record high of $850 per ounce and that this is likely to transpire between now and 1990.

As this book goes to press, gold is trading just above $450 an ounce, a level at which it is highly profitable to mine gold—and often even more profitable to discover it. Many of the stocks reviewed in Appendix I will produce substantial profits if gold only moves sideways. As should be obvious, if the gold price conforms to my expectations, as a group these stocks will do even better than the metal itself. And if this cycle is at all like its predecessors, most of us will be genuinely surprised by the performance of gold over the next few years—and significantly more surprised by the effects of record gold prices on all precious metals mining stocks.

While I expect gold to continue to function as the ultimate store of value as it has for many centuries and through countless currencies, I also expect that the time will come during the next few years when it will again make sense to abandon gold as an investment vehicle. Investors in gold and in all gold-related assets are rewarded for their opinions only if they take profits. No rewards go to those who are accurate in their assessment of gold's trend but fail to isolate the profits generated by their correct points of view.

The chief premise underlying my views on gold is that gold must rise in a financial environment that subsists on debt. Traditionally, societies that live on borrowed money are inevitably living on borrowed time. There's little about events occurring today to convince me that a break with tradition is imminent. Gold's steady rise since the February 1985 lows, the recent upside breakouts in terms of other major currencies (specifically, the yen, deutsche mark and Swiss franc), the inevitability of a decline in the Japanese stock market—and the maturity of the U.S. stock market—linked with the prospects of rising inflation suggest to me that gold will continue the established uptrend that is just now entering the dynamic phase of the cycle.

Many others see it differently. Two of the major arguments on behalf of the bearish scenario are worth considering, if only because they have received such widespread exposure. One view that many subscribe to is that gold is faking out investors, in much the same way it did coming off the lows in June 1982. This view was especially prominent early in 1987, when gold hit $480 and gold's detractors said it was only luring investors into the market for yet another

false start. While there's plenty of room for technical dis-
agreement on the similarities between gold today and gold
during the "mini-bull" market of 1982-83, the fundamental
similarities escape me entirely.

At that time, a gold bull market was fresh in the minds of
investors, whose eagerness to see a repeat drew them back
into the gold market with a vengeance. Although double-
digit inflation was recent history, deflationary trends were
already firmly in place, reinforced by high interest rates, a
strong dollar and falling commodity prices. In the fall of
1982, the Mexican debt crisis served as a primary catalyst
for the short-lived flurry in the gold market and was also the
first inkling many people had that there might be some paper
of dubious quality circulating in the international markets. In
the United States at the time, an immensely popular president
was perceived as doing what was necessary to put an end to
inflation. After two and a half years of a declining market, it
could also be argued that gold was entitled to a bounce to the
upside.

Today, an inflationary psychology—and a wildly bullish
gold market—are events not even remembered by most investors. On the contrary, the majority of people seem only to
remember that gold was once $850—and that it's selling for
about half that price today. The deflationary trends in place
in the early years of this decade have given way to rising
commodity prices and, given the magnitude of the drop in oil
prices and their subsequent recovery to the $18-$20 range, it
seems highly improbable that the best news on disinflation is
not already behind us.

As for the dubious quality of much of the world's debt,
it long ago became an accepted fact but still doesn't negate
the long-term consequences of defaults on existing loans and
on a world grown accustomed to living beyond its means.
The president who provided such a sharp contrast to his
predecessor and inspired confidence while presiding over the

biggest expansion of debt in our history is now crippled and ineffectual—the lamest of lame ducks.

Finally, in sharp contrast to the six-month bounce off the 1982 low in gold, the technical picture of today's gold market reveals an uptrend that remains firmly intact.

The fundamental contrasts I've noted suggest two very different financial environments, even allowing for my admitted tendency to wear gold-colored glasses. But setting aside the fundamentals, the comparison of the previous false start in gold to the current market seems even more compelling. Then, the market peaked only eight months off the June 1982 low; today, the slow but steady rise has 31 months of a constructive rising market behind it. At that, the market is on solid support and appears poised to continue the firmly established, albeit unexciting, trend. In my view, there's plenty of time for excitement later—but not for those who dismiss today's market as a repeat of its flash-in-the-pan predecessor.

Too Much Gold?

The other major argument offered by those who endorse a bearish scenario is the belief that the world is on the verge of a market glut that holds ominous implications for the price of gold. Several years from now, I think that's distinctly possible. Farmers have been victims of their own success at producing food at low costs and, in the realm of mineral commodities, the cycle of success breeding failure is well documented: uranium, molybdenum, copper and, more recently, silver, have all made the transformation from scarcity to relative abundance—and endured corresponding declines in price. Rising supplies of gold, it's lately become almost fashionable to argue, are on the verge of producing a similar result.

With all this gold around, it certainly begs the question: Why has the price of gold been rising for the past 31 months? While a review of new supplies can be a sobering experience to anyone who owns gold in hopes of making a profit, a look at demand helps to explain why the market has been rising, in spite of increased supplies. As *Barron's* recently pointed out, "Bulls on gold shrug off production gains, but eagerly discern growth in demand." Some gold bugs cited in the article suggested that, unlike other commodities, gold was somehow immune to the laws of supply and demand.

While gold *does* periodically take leave of the fundamentals, it's critical to an understanding of the yellow metal to realize that too much gold is not the same as too much wheat. And although gold's detractors often dismiss it as just another commodity, gold is different in several key respects:

1. Unlike virtually all other commodities, gold is a concentrated storehouse of wealth.

2. The relative quantity of historical production is exceedingly small in comparison to other commodities.

3. Gold is money and has a centuries-long track record to support that claim.

4. Gold is *the* commodity people flee to in times of financial crisis.

Whether a precious metal is owned for insurance or profit, it is reason number four, the "flee factor," that took gold to $850, silver to $50 and platinum to $1,050 in the last bull market. In the current bull market, which I believe has only just begun, it won't be routine supply and demand that will take all three metals to whatever heights they may attain: as in the past, it will be fear, greed, unknown events that lend themselves more to fortune telling than analysis and a host of other emotions that always seem to drive gold during times of crisis.

Investment demand is an intangible component of the gold price that's impossible to predict and foolhardy to underestimate. Given the lead time involved to put a gold mine into production, one would think that gold production could be predicted with reasonable accuracy. The *Gold Fields Study* is generally regarded as the most authoritative of the various annual reviews of the gold market, but even previous editions of this review have grossly underestimated the increased levels of gold production. If *Gold Fields* can't accurately predict supply, how can it—or anyone else—be expected to predict demand, an inherently more elusive part of the equation?

As has been the case in the platinum market in every year since 1981, investment demand can also play a critical role in determining gold's price. In the case of gold, platinum and silver, investment demand is a component that I believe has not even begun to have the impact that it will achieve over the next few years. More important, if each of these markets can rise in a noninflationary environment—as they have been doing—and in competition with a record-breaking stock market, what will happen when the general investing populace decides that owning some gold just might be a good idea?

Like all other commodities, gold vacillates between being in and out of favor. In my view, gold is only now on the threshold of being in favor once again. While trends in gold production aren't going to erase gold's historical role as an enduring store of value, I agree with *Barron's* that an oversupply of gold may be a real problem. We differ on our timetables, however; my guess is that *Barron's* speculation is a few years too early and that investment demand will once again prove to be the loose cannon that it has been in the past. Why? Because money is being created at a much faster pace in Washington than it is coming out of the ground in the Nevada desert, from the epithermal arc in the South

Pacific or from beneath the Canadian Shield. Until and unless that changes, gold will continue to be the beneficiary of our society's penchant for immediate gratification. For those who share that sentiment, precious metals mining stocks will again prove to be an exceedingly lucrative way to participate in the developing bull market in gold.

When *Barron's* and some of the others decide that rising gold production can be readily absorbed and that the gold market has been revalued in a lasting manner, my advice to investors would be to part with their own supply of gold, gold stocks and all other gold-related investment vehicles. In the meantime, gold seems to be doing just fine in spite of the glut.

Appendix I

Stock Recommendations

"Planned obsolescence" is a phrase that's perhaps best known for its applicability to automobiles, but it applies to stock recommendations as well. As prices rise, yesterday's favorites—one hopes all selling at higher prices—yield to new and lower-priced stocks, where the greatest potential for price appreciation traditionally lies.

It is for this reason that I've weighted my grouping of the reviews of the 25 companies that follow. Exploration companies that meet with a measure of technical success—or are merely blessed by a good market—have inherent upside potential; the best of the lot will be the development companies of tomorrow. A few of these companies are associated with other companies I would have recommended a year ago but that have since left the realm of penny stocks. Others were recommended in *Penny Mining Stock Report* in one category and have since progressed to the next stage, where they still merit purchase—but for different reasons now than they did before.

Before purchasing any of these stocks, I recommend you check prices against those preceding each company review. *Do not buy irrespective of price, as what may have been a good buy at $1 may be greatly overvalued at $2 or $3.* The volatility of the markets in penny mining shares poses problems getting current prices to newsletter subscribers, but this problem is greatly magnified in a book. I regarded the stocks that follow as good buys when this book went to press; subsequent developments may change my (your) outlook.

The prices that accompany each listing are current as of October 2, 1987; the number of shares are listed on a fully diluted basis and will also change as companies issue new shares to finance projects.* As this goes to press, I own shares in the following companies: Freewest, Geddes, Normine and Perron Gold. I mention this solely in the interest of disclosure and may not hold these positions when you read this book.

The stock symbols follow the heading of each review, with "V" denoting Vancouver, "T" signifying a Toronto listing and "M" indicating Montreal. *All stock prices and dollar figures are given in Canadian funds, unless noted otherwise.*

---

* Although this book was written in August 1987, prices were updated at press time and reflect prices before the stock market plunged on October 19, 1987. Because of the current volatility of the markets, prices may change dramatically by the time you read this.

Exploration-Stage Companies

Almaden Resources Corp. (V:AMH)

Fully diluted: 3,973,029
Price: $1.80

Almaden Resources is an exploration company with a portfolio of gold and silver properties, managed by a geological engineer with one of the most impressive track records in the Vancouver market. Duane Poliquin formed Westley Mines in 1972, sold control of the company in 1981 at a premium for himself and other shareholders and then went on to acquire and develop a former copper producer in Utah. That property, the Apex, is now held by Musto Explorations and is the only primary producer of germanium/gallium in the world. After spending the last several years in semiretirement, Poliquin brought Almaden public in October 1986. It is his only active involvement with a public company.

Apart from management's distinguished track record, Almaden has a broad exposure to exploration properties. In terms of exploration potential, the company's most significant holding is 500 square miles spread among three separate claim blocks in southeastern Manitoba. Almaden holds a 100 percent interest in 140 square miles of this large land position. An airborne survey program was completed in June 1987 and targets will be drill tested through the summer and fall.

The land retained by Almaden was explored for base metals in 1962 and good indications of gold values were found at that time. Subsequent aeromagnetic studies have shown that the geological environment that hosts the numerous gold occurrences of the Kenora, Ont., region continue into Manitoba and on into Minnesota. The Trans-Canada Highway adjoins the property and all necessary infrastructure is in place.

On the south claim block of this property group, Almaden recently entered into a joint venture with Granges Resources. For the expenditure of $2 million, Granges may earn a 60 percent interest in this property. On the north block, known as the Falcon Lake claims, Polestar Exploration Inc. can earn a 50 percent interest for the expenditure of $1.6 million. Should a mine result from the joint venture's efforts, Almaden will become the operator of the project.

With Pecos Resources, a wholly owned subsidiary of Granges Exploration, Almaden is exploring the Broken Hills silver property near Gabbs, in Mineral County, Nev. This property encompasses a former high-grade silver producer and Almaden is currently generating drill targets. The goal of this program is to develop a small, high-grade silver mine.

Another recent addition to Almaden is an agreement with Steep Rock Resources whereby Almaden may acquire a 100 percent interest in a 166-claim block in the King Bay, Sturgeon Lake area of Ontario. Almaden must spend $70,000 in drilling and metallurgy before September 15, 1989, and may buy Steep Rock's interest for $300,000 and 100,000 shares of Almaden stock. Previous drilling has indicated a near-surface gold-bearing zone and Almaden will examine the property with the hope of developing the deposit. Four new gold zones have been discovered and numerous drill targets have been located. Metallurgical work conducted by Almaden indicates gold recoveries in excess of 90 percent.

At Manitoba's Elbow Lake, the company recently entered into a joint venture with Westfield Minerals on a gold property in an area that encompasses geology similar to the Tartan Lake and Puffy Lake gold mines.

Finally, a work program will be conducted at the company's Munro Lake silver property, near Osoyoos, B.C. The company's broad array of prospects and numerous active programs ensure that investors will have many opportunities for upside potential in Almaden shares.

(Almaden Resources Corp., 475 Howe St., Suite 807, Vancouver, BC V6C 2B3, 604-689-7644.)

Arbor Resources (V, M:AOR)

Fully diluted: 12,100,000
Price: $3.05

Arbor Resources is the holding company of the Hughes-Lang group. AOR's major stock holding is a 3.1-million-share block of Perron Gold Mines. In view of the favorable prospects for production at Perron and what I believe are excellent prospects for upside appreciation, the Perron holdings must be viewed as a significant asset.

Arbor's primary focus of exploration is the Lone Star property, located approximately 10 miles south of Dawson City, Yukon. The Lone Star ground is situated between Bonanza and Eldorado Creeks, the two richest placer creeks in the Klondike gold fields, where combined production was in excess of 5 million ounces. The source of this placer gold has never been located, and the search for it is the focus of Arbor's program.

The company's 1986 exploration program included 13,000 feet of diamond and rotary drilling and encouraging gold assays were obtained from two zones. Significant gold-bearing intersections were encountered in several holes, and a $400,000 exploration program is planned for the 1987 field season. Arbor is earning a 60 percent interest in the property, after which the claims will be operated on a joint venture basis with Dawson-Eldorado Mines of Calgary. This project must be described as high-risk exploration, even in light of the good results obtained to date, but the potential rewards associated with success on this project could prove to be substantial.

Arbor's most advanced project is in Barraute Township, Queb., where Arbor and sister company Kangeld Resources have earned a 51 percent interest from Barexor Minerals Inc. This 1,122-acre gold property is the site of a $4 million program in 1987, with most of this expense directed toward underground exploration and development. A 10,000-foot surface and underground drilling program is under way and a 30,000-ton bulk sampling program is planned for later in the year.

Other Arbor properties include a 50 percent interest in 96 claims six miles east of the main ore structures at Perron Gold Mines' Chaste Township property. Arbor is spending $2 million and purchasing shares in Perron to earn its 50 percent interest. Arbor also has optioned the right to acquire a 100 percent interest in a 4,840-acre gold property in Madoc and Elzevir Township, one mile west of Queensborough, Ont. In addition to the large block of Perron shares, Arbor holds investment positions in nine other companies, most of them also in the Hughes-Lang group.

With one property at an advanced stage of development, several others showing signs of encouragement and major investments in other companies—especially Perron—Arbor is unusually diversified for an exploration company. I'm betting that their "many-irons-in-the-fire" approach will reward Arbor shareholders in the months and years ahead.

(Arbor Resources Inc., Suite 1900, 999 W. Hastings St., Vancouver, BC V6C 2W2, 604-687-6600.)

Arizona Star Resource Corp. (V:AZS)

Fully diluted: 4,618,800
Price: $1.65

Arizona Star is developing heap-leachable gold reserves on the Van Deemen property in the Black Mountains of northwestern Arizona. Historical production in this range is approximately 2.5 million ounces, principally from the Oatman and Union Pass districts to the south. The Van Deemen property hosts a detachment-fault-related gold deposit that bears a geological similarity to other gold producers in the region: Gold Fields' Mesquite mine, Glamis' Picacho and Eastmaque's Cargo Muchacho mine.

In April 1987, Amir Mines completed a private placement in Arizona Star, thus acquiring a controlling interest in AZS. Amir purchased 1.2 million shares for $.72 per share and holds options for an additional 1.2 million shares, which, if exercised, will result in Amir owning more than 50 percent of Arizona Star. Amir now has two out of five seats on the AZS board of directors and, more important, will no doubt be bringing other projects to the company. The exploration credentials of the Amir/Normine/Bema International group of companies have resulted in joint ventures with Glamis Gold and Kerr-Addison Mines; I don't think it requires much imagination to conclude that these associations will also eventually work to the benefit of Arizona Star and its shareholders.

The private placement of $864,000 will be used by Arizona Star to complete the earn-in of a 50 percent interest and to make additional acquisitions for the company. To date, AZS has developed drill-indicated and inferred reserves of 2 million tons of gold grading 0.042 ounces of gold per ton. The company estimates that reserves of up to 10 million tons are possible from the property's five known gold zones. A second-phase program of 10,000 feet of reverse circulation drilling is now under way. Preliminary stripping ratio calculations, leachability of the ore and environmental considerations are all positive, and the possibility of attaining near-term production appears excellent.

Arizona Star has a property of significant merit and is selling for substantially less than its April high of $2.15. The Amir connection was responsible for that high and, I believe, will be largely responsible for the development success of AZS and for any acquisitions made by the company. The greatest gains will be made by those who own the stock in advance of these developments.

(Arizona Star Resource Corp., 810-800 W. Pender St., Vancouver, BC V6C 2V6, 604-685-8844.)

Bema International Resources, Inc. (V:BMI)

Fully diluted: 3,950,000
Price: $4.05

Bema International is one of the companies in the Amir-Normine group, two related companies in joint venture with Glamis Gold on a gold belt in central Idaho. Bema management's expertise is in exploration, and the association of Amir and Normine with Glamis has produced one property that's currently the subject of test production, significant exposure to other gold properties in Idaho and a joint venture with Glamis on a large (2,400 acres) gold property in eastern Imperial County, Calif. This ground is in the eastern portion of the mineralized belt that extends from Gold Fields' Mesquite mine to Glamis' Picacho mine. Amir's sister company, Normine, is involved in a joint venture with Keradamex on the Slumbering Hills property adjoining Amax's Sleeper mine, near Winnemucca, Nev. Amir and Normine have been significant market successes and both companies' programs are well funded. Bema is the next generation.

Bema International became a public company on July 7, 1987, with the sale of 800,000 shares at $1. Bema is a consortium of companies consisting of Bema Industries, an exploration company; Teck Corp., a senior Canadian mining company; and Wright Engineers, Canada's pre-eminent mining engineering firm. Bema's primary focus is on a gold property near Harrison Lake, B.C. Bema is earning a 35 percent working interest for the expenditure of $1 million in 1987 and 1988, with joint venture partner and project operator Kerr-Addison Mines Ltd. holding a 25 percent working interest. Abo Resources holds the remaining 40 percent, also a working interest.

The Harrison Lake property has been the scene of 600 feet of underground development on the Jenner stock, one of eight intrusive stocks (ore-bearing structures) known to exist on the property. Previous work on the property has indicated that the Jenner stock alone could host 3-5 million tons of gold-bearing quartz diorite. The exploration program conducted by Kerr-Addison has shown that the results of previous drilling programs have significantly understated the gold content of the Jenner stock. The gold occurs in high-grade concentrations and presents an extreme nugget effect.

Underground sampling through August 1987 reported 290.1 feet of gold grading 0.142 ounces of gold per ton, with the mineralized zone open in all directions. Three underground raises are being driven into previously drilled areas and bulk samples to determine gold content will be taken from this work.

Although this project must be viewed as preliminary, the increased grade and the success of exploration to date suggest that the property is likely to be capable of supporting a positive production decision. If the results of the bulk sampling program are positive, a feasibility study by mid-1988 and production by mid-1989 would appear to be attainable. Preliminary estimates are that the property is capable of supporting a 1,500- to 2,000-ton-per-day mill; the deposit would be mined by the low-cost block-caving method.

In addition to the Harrison Lake property, Bema has been in negotiations with the China National Non-Ferrous Metals Corp. A proposed joint venture between the two groups has been narrowed down to the Liu Jia Ping-Golden Triangle in southwestern Shaanxi Province. Numerous massive sulfide deposits in the area have been delineated in an area that is currently host to two producing mines. The Liu Jia Ping-Golden Triangle was selected after two years of examining six major mineral belts throughout China. Although Bema's involvement in China remains highly prospective at this time, the company appears to be in a position to have the first operating joint venture with the Chinese and should benefit accordingly from its early involvement in that country.

The Harrison Lake property and the proposed Chinese joint venture justify purchase of Bema at this time. Management is highly regarded and, with a recent $3 million private placement, the company is well funded. The possibility that Bema one day will emerge as the flagship of the Amir-Normine group of companies, a result that would appear to make sense from the standpoint of consolidating the varied activities and ownership interests of the group, only adds to the long-term prospective value of BMI stock.

(Bema International Resources, Inc., Box 9, 900-609 W. Hastings St., Vancouver, BC V6B 4W4, 604-681-2323.)

Carson Gold (V:CQG)

(Formerly Cal-Denver Resources)
Fully diluted: 2,500,000
Price: $1.10

Carson Gold is a recently reorganized company that formerly traded as Cal-Denver Resources. Carson is involved in gold exploration in Italy and has gold production from a Yukon placer operation. Cal-Denver, the predecessor company, lost heavily as a result of the downturn in oil prices, necessitating a 1-for-2 share rollback.

Despite the disappointing stock performance throughout most of the four years I've been acquainted with the company, I've always liked management and currently like what I see in the company's Italian gold project. Spread over three separate districts in central and northern Italy, one of them the site of previous mercury production, initial sampling on this combined block of 24,000 acres have yielded excellent gold values. Several prospective joint venture partners—all major mining companies—are examining the properties.

Although preliminary in nature, the initial sampling programs and previous mercury production on one of the properties make this large land position an excellent target for the discovery of an epithermal gold deposit.

In addition to the large exploration program in Italy, Carson Gold also has a Yukon placer operation outside of Dawson City, equipment paid for by last year's production and an estimated 4,000 ounces of gold expected in the 1987 season.

(Carson Gold, 201 1512 Yew St., Vancouver, BC V6K 3E4, 604-731-1094.)

Channel Resources Ltd. (V:CHU)

Fully diluted: 4,700,000
Price: $3.80

It's a rare grassroots exploration company that I'll tell people to spend $4 on, but Channel is such an exception. A sister company to neighboring landholder Viceroy Resource, Channel is also headed by Viceroy's Ross Fitzpatrick. Before his involvement with Viceroy, Fitzpatrick was president of Westmount Resources. He sold out for a premium during an unfriendly takeover—before the debacle in the oil market—and in less than two years took Viceroy from a market capitalization of $3.5 million to a high of $375 million—and 24 million tons of gold grading 0.06 ounces of gold per ton.

In response to exploration success at the property, Hemlo Gold recently took a $25 million private placement in Viceroy. Fitzpatrick is a proven builder of companies and the acquisition of the company's Hackberry Mountain gold property makes me even more willing to bet on him.

The Hackberry claim block is located in the Hackberry Mountains, 18 miles south of Viceroy's Castle Mountain deposit. The area is the site of old workings that match the geological environment at Viceroy. While it's certainly premature to suggest that Channel will be "son of Viceroy," the same people think the Hackberry claims look a lot like Viceroy did a few years—and 1.5 million ounces—ago.

Subsequent to the acquisition of the property, eight grab samples averaged 0.049 ounces of gold per ton and a program of sampling and rotary drilling were scheduled for July 1987. The presence of gold, favorable geology and a large land position make this property interesting; the Viceroy connection ensures that the company's programs will be well funded and that market visibility will be high. I believe the Fitzpatrick/Viceroy factor justifies the premium currently reflected in the price of Channel shares.

(Channel Resources, 999 W. Hastings St., Suite 880, Vancouver, BC V6C 2W2, 604-688-9780.)

Cream Silver Mines Ltd. (V:CEM)

Fully diluted: 10,200,000
Price: $2.75

Incorporated in 1966, Cream Silver was the first of what is now known as the Hughes-Lang group of companies. Cream holds an interest in 106 claims on Vancouver Island, adjacent to Westmin Resources' 3,000-ton-per-day gold/silver/copper/lead/zinc mine and Cream's property finally will be the object of an exploration program in 1987. The Westmin and Cream properties are located on geologically similar ground and Cream's holdings are directly on strike of the Westmin ore bodies. Both properties are located in a provincial park and a mining moratorium was imposed on Cream's property in 1973. In January 1987, the B.C. government announced its intention to change the status to a recreational area, within which minerals exploration will be allowed. Cream will conduct preliminary geologic work to be followed by a late summer drilling program. Many regard this property as one of the best exploration targets in western Canada.

In northern British Columbia, Cream holds a substantial land position in the Atlin gold camp and has active exploration programs under way at this time. Cream also has a platinum prospect in the Thunder Bay district of northwestern Ontario, a 59-claim block adjoining Madeleine Mines' prospective platinum/palladium producer. The 1986 exploration program indicated significant platinum potential on Cream's Lac des Iles property. Numerous geochemical and geologic targets remain to be evaluated and a two-phase program of exploration, followed by drilling if warranted, is planned for 1987.

In addition to the precious/base-metals property on Vancouver Island and the Lac des Iles platinum property, CEM holds several other exploration properties: two separate claim blocks at Cameron Lake adjoining the Lockwood-Nuinsco project; the Garrison property, 67 miles east of Timmins, Ont.; 435 claims north of Abitibi Lake, Ont.; several prospective platinum claims in association with La Fosse Platinum; and a block of claims in the Dawson, Yukon, area, where the potential for large epithermal gold deposits is being tested by several other Hughes-Lang companies.

Cream's property on Vancouver Island must be viewed as an unusually high-potential property, its platinum property at Lac des Iles looks promising and the company has several other properties capable of generating news this year.

(Cream Silver Mines Ltd., 999 W. Hastings St., Suite 1900, Vancouver, BC V6C 2W2, 604-687-6600.)

Equinox Resources Ltd. (V, T:EQX)

Fully diluted: 4,700,000
Price: $4

Equinox Resources is an exploration-stage company with an unusually broad exposure to gold properties, a 40 percent interest in what is arguably the best portfolio of platinum properties in North America and a share in the production of a Nevada gold mine, the Buckhorn, a 38,000-ounce heap-leach gold producer.

Equinox's exposure to platinum represents its greatest market appeal and probably its highest potential should the company be involved in a significant discovery. Equinox has a 40 percent interest in and is the operator of programs on 18 platinum properties, all of them in a joint venture with Technigen Platinum. A total of $1.16 million will be spent on these properties during 1987.

Among the platinum properties, a 60-square-mile block of claims in the Muskox Intrusive Complex in the Northwest Territories must be regarded as the most promising. Platinum group metals are well documented in this area and the "Muskox Reef" is considered to be more similar to South

Africa's Merensky Reef than any other property known to exist in Canada.

Also high on the list of platinum exploration targets is the 36-claim block in the core of the Lac des Iles intrusive complex, which contains Canada's largest known platinum deposit. A total of $1.16 million will be spent on the company's platinum activities in 1987, with three properties being drilled.

In addition to platinum, EQX management believes that lithium will outperform most other metals during the next decade, largely due to increased demand from the battery and aerospace alloy markets. The company's main focus is on the Erex properties near Yellowknife, Northwest Territories, where joint venture partner LICO Resources can earn a 44 percent interest by spending $2.5 million over the next two years. Work on this 67-claim block during 1985 resulted in these claims being converted to a 21-year mining lease. With Teck Corp., Equinox is exploring the southwestern United States for lithium brine deposits, saline groundwater enriched with lithium.

Gallium and germanium are also the focus of EQX exploration programs. The company holds a 100 percent interest in the Cay property in British Columbia, where initial results suggested extremely high-grade concentrations of gallium, germanium and zinc. The company has interests in two other gallium/germanium properties and recently acquired a 50 percent interest in the Sunlight basin sulfur deposit in Park County, Wyo. This property contains a number of surface sulfur deposits and potential exists for a 5-million-ton deposit.

To enhance cash flow and build shareholder value for the long term, the company has been seeking the acquisition of an advanced or producing resource property. Equinox's capable management, its "many-irons-in-the-fire" approach to exploration and the almost complete absence of promotion should combine to build a strong asset base—and higher stock prices—over the long term.

(Equinox Resources Ltd., 500-576 Seymour St., Vancouver, BC V6B 5K1, 604-684-1175.)

Freewest Resources Inc. (M:FWE)

Fully diluted: 2,644,600
Price: $2.59

Freewest is a May 1987 listing on the Montreal Stock Exchange with several interesting gold properties and some platinum properties that have yielded good values and favorable ratios of platinum to palladium. In Collet and Laberge townships, just south of the Inco-Golden Knight discovery in Casa Berardi Township, FWE has 80 claims on which the results of a recent diamond drilling program are awaited. The company also is earning a 30 percent interest in the Cline Lake property, held jointly by Cline (40 percent) and Noranda (currently 60 percent, diluting to 30 percent). Results of a first-phase drilling program were highly encouraging and a $400,000 followup drilling program was scheduled to begin in July 1987.

Also in joint venture with Noranda, FWE recently concluded an agreement that would allow the company to earn up to a 42 percent interest in a Harker-Holloway Township property, just east of the east zone of a Canamax property with published reserves of 578,000 tons grading 0.246 ounces of gold per ton. The Freewest/ Noranda property has known gold values and a first-phase drilling program is scheduled.

In addition to gold, Freewest has two platinum exploration properties. The Lac des Montagnes property has been undergoing a geochemical survey and trenching program in preparation for a fall drilling program. This property has reported values of platinum/ palladium and an occurrence of chromite that shows promise. Near Fort Frances, Ont., Freewest recently acquired the right to earn a 100 percent interest in an old Noranda property from two local prospectors who restaked it. Five recent grab samples yielded combined platinum/palladium values of 0.13 ounces per ton, with favorable 2-to-1 ratios of palladium to platinum.

Although grassroots in nature, FWE has experienced management, several good properties and appears well positioned to benefit from the results of the 1987 exploration season.

(Freewest Resources, Inc., 800 Dorchester West, Suite 1525, Montreal, PQ H3B 1X9, 514-878-3551.)

Geddes Resources (V:GDD)

Fully diluted: 7,100,000
Price: $3.90

Geddes Resources is a Toronto-based minerals exploration company with a 100 percent interest in the Windy Craggy volcanogenic massive sulfide deposit located in the St. Elias Mountains of northwestern B.C. Exploration programs conducted by Falconbridge Ltd. (which retains a 22.5 percent net profits interest) over the past 30 years have outlined a mineral discovery of worldclass proportions. Drilling to date has identified 100 million tons of massive sulfides with an average grade of 2.4 percent copper and approximately two pounds of cobalt per ton, plus gold, silver and zinc values.

The deposit has a strike length of 6,000 feet and drilling has indicated massive sulfides to a depth of 1,600 feet and a width of 400 feet. Within this massive deposit, drilling has identified an area where the sulfide body narrows and significant gold values were encountered. A single drill hole within this zone revealed the potential for much higher gold grades than were encountered elsewhere in the deposit: 201 feet grading 0.290 ounces of gold per ton over a true width of 160 feet, including 127 feet grading 0.370 ounces of gold per ton and 20 feet grading 1.0 ounces of gold per ton.

Geddes is gaining access to the gold zone through a 5,500-foot adit, currently being driven to the gold zone. A minimum of 10,000 feet of diamond drilling will be undertaken to define this zone. Results from this drilling aren't likely to be available until late fall of 1987, but exploration of the company's nearby Tats showing, where high-grade copper has been found, may generate some news in the meantime. Surprises encountered in the driving of the adit may do likewise.

While Windy Craggy is known to be an immense mineral inventory of worldclass proportions, its viability as a gold deposit is more uncertain, hinging on this one, albeit spectacular, hole. With the deposit's large widths and a gravity mining system with adit access, it's not difficult to see GDD becoming an extremely low-cost gold producer.

If the gold exploration program continues to prove successful, Windy Craggy will be developed as a gold mine and in later years will almost certainly be a copper and cobalt producer. This is likely to happen only if the necessary infrastructure for a gold mine is first put in place. A 3,000-foot airstrip currently exists on the property; air access during the exploration season is excellent but can be a problem during the winter months. Road access, not a prerequisite for building a gold mine, will depend on the property's eventual development as a copper mine.

Geddes also holds 500,000 shares in Goldpost Resources, Inc., a former subsidiary company that holds or is earning interests in three gold properties in northern Ontario. Goldpost shares have shown substantial appreciation in the recent past and there is reason to believe that Geddes has an investment that will continue to rise in value.

In its Windy Craggy deposit, Geddes Resources has an asset of worldclass proportions whose long-term future will be determined by copper prices and gaining road access to the property. Near term, the company has a gold exploration property with one spectacular hole and the potential to be a major gold deposit with exceptionally low production costs. The deposit suggests the possibility of huge potential gains and merits a longer-term perspective—and higher profit objective—than in most exploration-stage companies.

(Geddes Resources, Ltd., Guinness Tower, 1080-1055 W. Hastings St., Vancouver, BC V6C 2W2, 604-682-2392.)

Gerle Gold Ltd. (V:GGL)

Fully diluted: 3,810,000
Price: $1

Gerle Gold typifies why investing in management is so important: the investor gets a second chance. I first recommended Gerle when some very high expectations were being factored into the price of its Happy Creek property, 40 miles northwest of Winnemucca, Nev. Initially, results were poor and the stock declined in sympathy. As much of the poor showing at Happy Creek was attributed to sampling problems, that property continues to look promising but, in the meantime, the company was also seeking acquisitions.

On June 1, 1987, the company announced a 50-50 joint venture with Mahogany Minerals, the object of exploration being the Frisco mine, a former gold producer in Mohave County, Ariz. The Frisco is located nine miles east of Bullhead. Previous production was from a high-grade underground operation in the early 1900s and, between 1984 and 1986, from a 66,000-ton test pad that yielded gold recoveries of 70 percent and an average grade of 0.058 ounces of gold per ton. Subsequent to the acquisition of the property, bulk samples from an exposed ore zone returned much higher gold values; two other zones on the property remain to be drilled. Based on the encouraging initial results, the joint venture plans to accelerate the drilling program and begin the application process for a heap-leaching operation. The reserve potential of the property is estimated to be more than 10 million tons.

In addition to the Arizona property, Gerle has an option to earn a 100 percent interest in the Happy Creek property and owns outright the McConnell Creek gold property in the Omineca mining division in British Columbia. Gerle management believes that this property has the potential to develop into a large-tonnage gold deposit. Gerle also has an agreement in principle to acquire a 50 percent working interest in the Snowflake gold property in the Nicola mining district, also in British Columbia.

Gerle's broad portfolio of exploration properties is impressive and, with the acquisition of the prospective heap-leach producer in Arizona, the company could well be positioned to join the ranks of gold producers by 1988.

(Gerle Gold Ltd., 904-675 W. Hastings St., Vancouver, BC V6B 1N2, 604-688-3584.)

Golden Princess Mining Corp. (V:GLP)

(Formerly O.T. Industries)
Fully diluted: 4,650,226
Price: $1.40

Golden Princess is a Vancouver-based exploration-stage company characterized by an exceptionally strong management team and a portfolio of gold properties to match. Foremost among the company's gold projects is the Nickel Offsets property, 18 miles north of Timmins, Ont., and nine miles east of the famous Kidd Creek mine. The Timmins-Porcupine gold camp is one of the world's largest, with recorded production in excess of 54 million ounces of gold, second only to the Witwatersrand camp in South Africa. At Nickel Offsets, GLP may earn up to a 35 percent interest by funding a $3 million exploration program, to be managed by Noranda, GLP's joint venture partner.

Between 1969 and 1981, the former owners of the property drilled 54 holes, outlining 600,000 tons of reserves with an average grade of 0.23 ounces of gold per ton. Considerable exploration potential exists, as only 1,250 feet of a 1.5-mile gold-bearing structure have been tested. A 17,000-foot drilling program began in June 1987. In view of the known reserves on the property and the large areas of it that remain to be explored, the chances for reserve expansion are considered excellent.

Also in joint venture with Noranda, GLP holds a 50 percent interest in the Carnation property, a small former gold producer near Parker, in La Paz County, Ariz. The property is in the same geologic environment as several other producers, most notably Glamis Gold's Picacho mine and Consolidated Gold Fields' Mesquite mine. Noranda recently conducted a 17-hole reverse circulation drilling program to test for evidence of low-grade ore; having found economic mineralization in two separate areas of the property, the joint venture will proceed with a second-stage program beginning in May 1988.

Exploration will also be proceeding on the company's Dona Lake and Tarp Lake properties in the Pickle Lake region of northern Ontario, another area of prolific gold production. GLP has the option to earn a 49 percent interest by spending a total of $300,000 on exploration. A diamond drilling program began in May 1987 under the supervision of Kerr-Addison Mines, the holder of the remaining interest in the properties. In the Casa Berardi gold camp, Golden Princess has a sizable land position—2,800 acres—and negotiations are under way with a major mining company to further explore this property. Known as the Lac Raymond, this large group of claims is located one mile north of the Inco-Golden Knight property. Highly anomalous arsenic concentrations, which coincide with gold mineralization elsewhere in the district, are known to occur on the Lac Raymond property. The source of their occurrence will be the first objective of any exploration program.

In summary, Golden Princess management has acquired an impressive array of exploration properties, blue-chip joint venture partners and active programs on several properties that should give investors ample opportunities to profit from successful exploration programs. A recent private placement put the company's working capital in excess of $1 million and, in my view, suggests that influential market sponsorship bodes well for GLP shareholders. Given the breadth of experience of Golden Princess management, its advisors to the company and its broad exposure to mining properties in Canada and the United States, I think it's a safe bet that the company's current strong property portfolio will be enhanced in the future.

(Golden Princess Mining Corp., 475 Howe St., Suite 508, Vancouver, BC V6C 2B3, 604-688-6681.)

Goldstack Resources (V:GDR)

Fully diluted: 3,200,000
Price: $2

Goldstack Resources is an exploration-stage company with a Quebec property with a small reserve base and another property adjacent to a recent discovery, both of which will be the site of active programs in 1987. In Dubuisson Township, seven miles from Val d'Or, Sullivan Mines and Exploration Aumine are each earning a one-third interest in Goldstack's former Malartic Goldfields mine. Nine million tons of 0.17-ounce gold were mined and the current focus of exploration is an area of the mine that was drilled and partially developed before the mine was closed in the 1940s.

In Quebec's Duverny Township, adjacent to a recent discovery by Sphinx Explorations Inc., the Sphinx deposit has estimated reserves of 2 million tons grading 0.22 ounces of gold per ton. A prospective open-pit mine, the Sphinx deposit has been traced to the common boundary between it and the Goldstack property. Goldstack has purchased a 100 percent interest in the property for a cash payment of $100,000 and four equal payments over the next four years and is then subject to a 2 percent net smelter return. Another property, also located in Dubuisson Township, is optioned to Noranda Explorations and Noranda is spending $150,000 on it during the current season.The Dubuisson property where Sullivan is working to expand reserves has been the primary focus of the company and, from a property standpoint, has been almost the sole reason to own GDR.

(Goldstack Resources, 535 Sir Wilfred Laurier Blvd., Suite 316, Beloeil, PQ J3G 5E9, 514-467-2514.)

Interaction Resources Ltd. (V:INR)

Fully diluted: 6,304,482
Price: $1.95

Interaction Resources has an extensive portfolio of precious metals exploration properties in Nevada, California, Utah and British Columbia and producing oil and gas interests in the U.S. and Canada. Founded in 1979 as Intermet Resources, this is a company with an undistinguished history —but a recent past that now makes it worthy of purchase.

On June 3, 1987, the company announced the acquisition of the Fireball Ridge property, which is considered to be an excellent epithermal gold target. Recent changes in management, coupled with this new property acquisition, suggest that INR is a strong candidate for higher prices.

The Fireball Ridge property is located 55 miles northeast of Reno and consists of five square miles of deeded land and 68 unpatented claims. INR has the right to earn a 100 percent interest in the property, subject to a 6 percent net smelter return to the vendors. Cominco, the original owner, acquired its land position in 1985 and conducted mapping, rock-chip and soil sampling, limited geophysics, trenching and limited drilling on the property. A 1986 drilling program intersected grades of 0.196 ounces of gold per ton over 40 feet.

Preliminary drilling outlined a mineralized zone approximately 70 feet thick. The geology and structure of the property mimics that of AMAX's Sleeper gold mine and only a small portion of the 2.5-mile strike length of the Fireball fault has been explored. A geochemical survey and other preliminary geologic work was scheduled to conclude in a drilling program in late summer 1987.

Also in Nevada, Interaction is earning a 51 percent interest in the Mill property in the Battle Mountain mining district in Lander County, Nev. Bow Valley Industries Ltd. and Brican Resources Ltd. are the joint venture partners and the goal is to locate a Carlin-type gold deposit. Detailed geologic mapping and a reverse circulation drilling program are planned for the 1987 season.

Other properties include a 100 percent interest in a 40-claim block south of Goldfield, Nev., a bonanza lode target; a 100 percent interest in the Cuprite property, an epithermal target 15 miles south of Goldfield, where Homestake has staked all of the surrounding ground; and several other large-tonnage, open-pit targets in Nevada. The company's well-situated properties andrecent changes in management, bode well for the appreciation potential of INR shares.

(Interaction Resources Ltd., 720-800 W. Pender St., Vancouver, BC V6C 2V6, 604-684-2285.)

Lyon Lake Mines Ltd. (M:LLL)

Fully diluted: 3,561,000
Price: $2.40

Lyon Lake is a recent listing on the Montreal Stock Exchange (May 1987) with several advanced exploration properties and an ongoing search for a property with reserves. Lyon Lake Mines shares common management with Audrey Resources and both companies show excellent potential to make the transition from exploration to production.

Lyon Lake was formed by Falconbridge Ltd. in 1971 to conduct exploration programs, which it did until operations were suspended in 1976. Control of the company changed hands in 1980 but remained inactive until last year, when present management acquired control. Since then, LLL has been acquiring exploration properties and is, in effect, the exploration arm of Audrey Resources. Lyon Lake has an option to acquire a 50 percent interest in Audrey's Belleterre and Estrees-Estrades properties.

Lyon Lake must spend $1.25 million within three years at Belleterre, a 315-claim property in northwestern Quebec. This property represents the prospective extension of Quebec Belleterre Gold Mines, which produced 2 million tons with an average grade of 0.31 ounces of gold per ton. Surface samples on Lyon Lakes' property have yielded high-grade gold values and one drill hole indicated 0.24 ounces of gold per ton over a length of 1.5 meters. Several drill targets have been defined on this property and a 20,000-foot diamond drilling program was scheduled to begin in June 1987.

Located in the Casa-Berardi gold camp, Lyon Lake is conducting exploration programs totaling at least $750,000 over a three-year period. This 95-claim block in Estree and Estrades Townships is located in the same volcanic belt that hosts the Inco-Golden Knight deposit and the Golden Hope discovery. Last year, Audrey completed geophysical surveys that outlined the anomalies that are the targets of this year's exploration program. A 10,000-foot first-phase diamond drilling program was also scheduled to begin in 1987.

Another recent acquisition is the Carheil property, 158 claims in Carheil Township, southwest of the Selbaie mine. Recent aerial geophysical surveys are being evaluated to formulate an exploration program, for which $350,000 is budgeted in 1987.

Lyon Lake has an interesting portfolio of exploration projects, a goal of reserve acquisition and experienced management with a demonstrated track record of building value for shareholders. The company's low capitalization and numerous active exploration programs make Lyon Lake Mines an excellent candidate for share appreciation from current levels.

(Lyon Lake Mines Ltd., 70 Avenue du Lac, Rouyn-Noranda, PQ J9X 4N4, 819-764-9411.)

Mary Ellen Resources Ltd. (V:MYE)

Fully diluted: 4,533,100
Price: $1.85

Mary Ellen Resources is one of the Kasner group of companies, which includes Lenora, Argentex and Sholia, all managed by president Robert Kasner, a promoter with a solid track record of giving investors a run for their money. MYE is an exploration-stage company with multiproperty exposure to both gold and platinum, the latter being the primary reason to own shares in the company.

One of the best ways to make a mine is to look next door to an existing mine; another way is to "find" a mine where there used to be one, returning a former producer to production status. Still another way to locate a new mine is to take a geological model from one location and see if it applies to a similar geological environment in a different location. Based on the discovery of gold and platinum mineralization at the former Coronation Hill uranium mine in Australia, a similar type of deposit was targeted for discovery in the Beaverlodge mining camp of northern Saskatchewan, an area dominated by former uranium producers. Coronation Hill and the Beaverlodge region are of the same geologic age and the presence of gold/platinum mineralization in both areas has proven the existence of a new type of mineral deposit. Mary Ellen has interests in five separate properties in the Beaverlodge area, each of them containing known occurrences of gold and platinum. At Fishhook Bay, Mary Ellen is in joint venture with Eldor Resources and is earning a 40 percent interest by spending $1 million by August 15, 1987. At Nicholson Bay, MYE can earn a 60 percent interest from the Saskatchewan Mining Development Corp. by spending $500,000 on exploration. Both of these properties contain high-grade gold values and excellent grades of platinum group metals, with favorable ratios of platinum to palladium. Although preliminary in nature, the known occurrences of gold in association with platinum, coupled with the precedent of Coronation Hill, combine to make this an exciting project that will yield answers in the coming season.

In addition to the platinum story, Mary Ellen has interests in several gold exploration properties. Near Kirkland Lake, Ont., Mary Ellen holds a 100 percent interest in an 83-claim block located on the extension of the Larder Lake break, an area hosting several gold producers (Sigma, Kerr-Addison, Wright Hargreaves and Lakeshore Mines). In Harker and Holloway townships, also in Ontario, a joint venture between Mary Ellen and the Canadian Nickel Co. Ltd. is testing the downdip extension of the American Barrick Holt-McDermott discovery. Three million tons grading 0.20 ounces of gold per ton have been outlined and American Barrick recently announced a production decision. Preliminary results from a deep diamond drill hole program recently yielded a 9.1-foot intersection with an average grade of 0.37 ounces of gold per ton.

Mary Ellen has an unusually broad array of exploration properties, highlighted by its platinum program being conducted in the Beaverlodge area. The application of the Australian model to North America is likely to create a good deal of interest in this project and any degree of exploration success should ensure a much higher price for MYE shares. The additional exposure to gold on two fronts near proven deposits is not insignificant and could produce similar results. Mary Ellen has several chances for success and aggressive management that ensures the story will be told.

(Mary Ellen Resources Ltd., Box 546, Kirkland Lake, ON P2N 3L1, 705-642-3291.)

McAdam Resources, Inc. (T:MMM)

Fully diluted: 5,650,130
Price: $3.25

McAdam Resources is a company with two properties in advanced stages of exploration and management that is shared by two other companies, Muscocho and Flanagan McAdam. John McAdam, Jr. heads McAdam, which, like its sister company Flanagan McAdam, is an exploration-stage company, albeit at a less advanced stage.

McAdam has interests in two former gold producers, the McWatters property, near Rouyn, Queb., and the Spud Valley, on Vancouver Island off the British Columbia coast. The McWatters property is located on the Larder-Cadillac Break six miles southeast of Rouyn. The McWatters mine produced more than 100,000 ounces at a grade approximating 0.30 ounces of gold per ton. The previous owners estimated reserves up to 431,575 tons with an average grade of 0.193 ounces of gold per ton.

A drilling program to upgrade reserves is under way at McWatters, where McAdam is earning a 100 percent interest and Tashota-Nipigon Mines and Quinteko Resources are each earning 25 percent of McAdams' interest. With 16 holes drilled, 11 economic gold intersections have been encountered, the best of these grading 0.75 ounces of gold per ton over 16 feet. Near the old shaft, a recent hole graded 0.632 ounces of gold per ton over 18.4 feet. Two other recent holes, drilled 1,000 feet farther west than any previous holes, encountered the same zones. Tonnage-building potential at McWatters appears excellent. Dewatering to the 400-foot level is in progress and a diamond drilling program continues. With a small reserve base and all infrastructure in place at McWatters, McAdam is spending $6 million in the next 12 months toward making a production decision by the end of February 1988.

The company's 100-percent-owned Spud Valley property, in which Tashota-Nipigon is earning a 25 percent interest, is another former producer: approximately 54,000 ounces with an average grade of 0.29 ounces of gold per ton were mined from 1938-42 and economic-grade intersections have been encountered in the current diamond drilling program. Preliminary reserves are estimated at 429,000 tons averaging 0.253 ounces of gold per ton. Highlights of the ongoing drilling program include a 4.2-foot section that returned 3.2 ounces of gold per ton. McAdam's budget for Spud Valley is $1 million in 1987 and the surface drilling program is expected to move underground in the summer.

Unlike many exploration companies, McAdam has two advanced properties (both former producers), well-funded programs that will result in almost $7 million being spent on them and a management team that's highly regarded in the mining fraternity. Despite a capitalization that's higher than I generally like to see in exploration companies, the advanced stage of both projects and, more important, a small float (approximately 1.5 million) mitigates the number of shares outstanding (2.65 million shares are held by insiders, Muscocho and two gold funds). Based on the progress at both properties, I think McAdam is a buy at this time.

(McAdam Resources, Inc., 25 Adelaide St. East, Suite 1415, Toronto, ON M5C 1Y2, 416-362-9671.)

Normine Resources Ltd. (V:NON)

Fully diluted: 5,890,263
Price: $3.55

Normine is a company distinguished by its almost unique breadth of exposure to properties and its penchant for high-potential exploration targets. That's the upside potential; the downside is amply covered by the prospects of early gold production at the company's jointly held Idaho properties and by excellent management and strong joint venture partners. NON became a public company in May 1984, the outgrowth of management's ownership of Bema Industries, a respected exploration contracting firm. In that capacity, management gained experience on a wide variety of properties—held by majors and junior companies alike—and ultimately decided to do for themselves what they formerly did for others.

In the spring of 1986, after weathering some bad markets and unsuccessful properties, Normine formed a joint venture with sister company Amir Mines and with Glamis Gold, one of the pioneers of the heap-leach industry.

While the prospects of gold production in Idaho appear excellent and provide a strong base for the company, participation in the Wait project near Kimberley, B.C., provides the greatest potential for share appreciation. The significance of the Wait project is that it is located six miles east of Cominco's Sullivan mine, one of the world's largest massive sulfide deposits. NON is in the middle of a 10-hole diamond drilling program to test the source of several large gravity anomalies. NON can earn a 51 percent interest in the property by spending $1 million by December 31, 1988.

Other projects include the Goosly Lake property adjoining the Equity silver mine and a property adjoining the Bralorne and Pioneer mines, which together comprise the largest historical production in western Canada. Normine is highly respected for its exploration abilities and, even if the company's high-potential targets don't develop as exploration successes, management will undoubtedly acquire other properties of merit to explore.

(Normine Resources Ltd., Box 9, 609 W. Hastings St., Vancouver, BC V6B 4W4, 604-681-8371.)

Panorama Resources Ltd. (V:PMA)

Fully diluted: 4,300,000
Price: $3.50

Panorama Resources is another company formerly exploring for oil and gas that has recently switched to minerals exploration. In 1987, after reviewing several properties, management acquired two advanced-stage properties, the Spanish mine in California and the Platoro, a former gold/silver producer in Colorado. Drilling programs are underway at Spanish mine and an underground program at the Platuro, the objective in each case to sufficiently enlarge the reserve base to complete feasibility studies in 1988.

Located in the San Juan mountains of southern Colorado, about four miles from Summitville, the Platoro mine was discovered in the 1890s and produced into the early 1900s. In the 1960s and mid-70s, a small milling operation recovered 4,900 ounces of gold and 172,000 ounces of silver. The 19,500-acre Platoro property was acquired in 1979 by Union Mines, the U.S. subsidiary of Union Miniere, the Belgian metals conglomerate. Since then Union has spent $18 million on 65,000 feet of diamond drilling and 9,000 feet of underground workings. According to an agreement in August 1987, Panorama may earn up to a 60 percnt interest for the expenditure of $8 million, with Panorama the operator of the project.

Panorama's aim is to block out 500,000-750,000 tons of ore from a geologically indicated reserve of 3 million tons of 0.25 ounces of gold equivalent per ton, an estimate based on a study by consultants Pincock, Allen and Holt. The Mammoth-Revenue vein averages eight to ten feet in width and has a defined strike length of 11,000 feet, with the prospects for expanding this considered excellent.

The company's other property of merit is the Spanish mine, 2,000 acres of patented and unpatented mining claims in Nevada County, Calif. Located about 20 miles east of Grass Valley, the Spanish mine first produced from an open pit in 1883 and was the site of a high-grade underground mine in the 1930s. In the early 1980s, Homestake Mining Co. carried out a program of geological mapping, surface channel sampling and diamond drilling. Approximately 700,000 tons of oxidized material grading 0.12 ounces of gold per ton were outlined by Homestake's drilling; PMA's exploration goal is to expand these reserves. Previous mining activities have indicated a gold system up to 150 feet thick and more than two miles long. Should the property support a production decision, the deposit would be an open-pit operation. Metallurgical testing has already demonstrated the amenability of the ore to heap leaching.

Panorama president John Dreier is highly regarded in the mining fraternity, and enjoys the sponsorship of one of Vancouver's best brokers, Canarim's Ray Saadien. The combination of people and two advanced-stage properties—and my strong belief that PMA will only move higher—makes this company a low-risk investment on the scale of junior mining companies.

(Panorama Resources Ltd., 808 10th St., Golden, CO 80401, 303-279-1904.)

Development Companies

Amir Mines (V, T:AMM)

Fully diluted: 5,900,000
Price: $4.65

Since its formation as a public company in 1983, Amir has made the transition from a grassroots exploration company to developing gold producer. In June 1986, Amir entered into a joint venture with heap-leach pioneer Glamis Gold, which will allow Glamis to earn a 51 percent interest in the Buffalo Gulch property near Elk City, Idaho, and fund all exploration and development costs.

Also in Idaho, in the same gold belt, Amir, Glamis and sister company Normine Resources share an interest (24 percent, 51 percent and 25 percent, respectively) in the Buffalo Gulch north deposit. A detailed reverse-circulation drilling program during the 1986 season outlined proven and probable reserves of 5 million tons with an average grade of 0.03 ounces of gold per ton and potential for an additional 3 million tons of similar-grade material. Although low in grade, the friable nature of the ore and high gold recoveries in preliminary metallurgical tests suggest that this property also will be amenable to low-cost gold production. In the same gold belt, the Friday property has proven and probable reserves approximating 3 million tons averaging 0.04 ounces of gold per ton; preliminary results yielded high gold recoveries during a short leach cycle and bulk leach testing is under way at this time. A substantial amount of property within the belt remains to be explored.

Two recent developments add a new dimension to the company's ongoing exploration programs in Idaho. In early April, Amir announced the acquisition of a controlling position in Arizona Star Resource Corp., a Vancouver company exploring the Van Deemen claim group near Kingman, Ariz. This property is in the same geological environment that hosts Consolidated Gold Fields' Mesquite property, Eastmaque Mines' Cargo Muchacho mine and Glamis Gold's Picacho mine.

In June 1987, Amir and Glamis announced a joint venture (35 percent/65 percent) also in the same area, on 2,400 claims in eastern Imperial County, acquired by Glamis from Gold Fields Mining Corp. These claims cover a 75-mile area extending over the eastern portion of the mineralized belt that runs from Gold Fields' Mesquite deposit to Glamis' Picacho mine. Amir will be the operator for all exploration and Glamis will be the operator on all development and production.

Amir's exploration talents, coupled with the demonstrated abilities of Glamis to produce gold at low costs, lend an unusual degree of credibility to the company's programs. The prospect of imminent gold production and strong and growing support in the market suggest that Amir shareholders will be rewarded for their expression of confidence in managment.

(Amir Mines Ltd., 609 W. Hastings St., Suite 900, Vancouver, BC B6B 4W4, 604-681-8371.)

Flanagan McAdam Resources (T:FMR)

Fully diluted: 8,336,852
Price: $3.75

Flanagan McAdam, which shares common management with Muscocho Explorations, is an advanced exploration company whose primary holding is a 50 percent interest in the Magnacon gold property near Mishibishu Lake, Ont. Muscocho, the operator, holds a 25 percent interest, with Windarra Minerals holding the remaining 25 percent. This area has become one of Canada's most active regions of exploration and a $10.7 million program in 1987 assures investors a steady stream of drilling results—and opportunities for share appreciation. FMR is managed by the well-known team of John McAdam and Terry Flanagan. With Muscocho, they proved their ability to develop properties to production; with FMR, results of exploration to date suggest that they may be headed toward their second producing mine.

The Magnacon property is being explored from underground and results have been extremely encouraging. Gold values obtained underground have been substantially higher than grades indicated in the surface drilling program. In addition to excellent grades, there is substantial potential for reserve expansion. Two underground ramps are currently being advanced; one to open up a second level of the main zone, the other to gain access to the western extension zone 1,300 feet west of the main area. Preliminary estimates stand at 700,000 tons averaging 0.22 ounces of gold per ton.

At Gwillim Lake, FMR and Muscocho each hold a 43.3 percent interest in a 36-claim block in McKenzie Township in the Chibougamau district of Quebec. This property is located between two former gold producers and a $750,000 surface diamond drilling program is under way. Flanagan and Muscocho recently concluded an agreement whereby both companies can earn a 50 percent interest in the Gwillim Lake gold mine, which significantly expands the potential for this property.

Between their Magnacon project, the Gwillim Lake property and management that has earned the respect of the investment community, Flanagan McAdam shares hold considerable potential for appreciation.

(Flanagan McAdam Resources, 25 Adelaide St. East, Suite 601, Toronto, ON M5C 1Y2, 416-363-1124.)

Northair Mines Ltd. (V, T:NRM)

Fully diluted: 11,000,000
Price: $2.55

Northair is one of the Northair group of companies, all overseen by Don McLeod, a veteran of the Canadian mining scene who has put two mines into production and appears headed toward production on two others. One is a Northair-held property, the other is the Sulphurets property of sister company Newhawk Gold. Northair's primary focus is on the Willa property in southeastern British Columbia, where NRM is earning a 68 percent interest in joint venture with BP Selco and Rio Algom.

The company is in the final phase of exploration on this property, where reserves currently stand at approximately 600,000 tons grading 0.22 ounces of gold per ton, 0.33 ounces of silver per ton and 1.05 percent copper. A feasibility study will commence in the fall of 1987 and environmental hearings preparatory to a positive mining decision are under way. Given a positive feasibility study, Northair management believes the property can be placed into production by June 1988. The tentative plan calls for the relocation of the company's wholly owned Brandywine mill from the Brandywine mine site near Squamish, B.C. This mine operated from June 1976 until 1982, when low metals prices and declining ore grade forced its closure.

Also in joint venture with BP Selco, Northair is earning a 35 percent interest in an 84,000-acre gold target near Long Lake, Newfoundland. A detailed geochemical program, followed by trenching and, if indicated, a drilling program is scheduled to begin on this prospective open-pittable deposit.

It was announced in April 1987 that Northair was the object of a hostile takeover attempt by Nor-Quest Resources. Northair easily survived the takeover attempt and my guess is that a mine will be the likely outcome of the company's program at the Willa.

(Northair Mines Ltd., 625 Howe St., Suite 860, Vancouver, BC V6C 2T6, 604-687-7545.)

Rouyn Mining Resources Inc. (M, T:ROU)

Fully diluted: 8,500,000
Price: $6.37

Rouyn is developing three Quebec gold properties from which production is projected in 1988-89. The properties are all located within a five-mile radius, 12 miles west of Rouyn-Noranda, Que. Two of the properties, the Wasamac and the Francoeur, in joint venture with Lac Minerals, are former producers. Rouyn is the operator of all three projects. Preliminary estimates of total production at the three properties is 78,000 ounces annually, with cash production costs estimated at $200 (U.S.) per ounce. The company is debt-free and has exceptional management in the person of president Jean-Guy Rivard. Guy Hebert, president of Audrey Resources and Lyon Lake Mines, also serves on Rouyn's board.

Rivard is a Rouyn-Noranda businessman who acquired the company's 100-percent-owned Lac Fortune property in 1980 and incorporated Rouyn in 1981. Gold was discovered at Lac Fortune in 1906, where gold mineralization, as at the other properties, is structurally related to the Larder-Cadillac fault. Between 1910 and 1935, three shafts were sunk on the property and extensive underground work was conducted. Since 1984, Rouyn has developed 247,385 tons grading 0.157 ounces of gold per ton. A $1 million program to expand reserves is currently under way at Lac Fortune.

At the company's Francoeur project, probable and possible reserves total 2.25 million tons with an average grade of 0.198 ounces of gold per ton. The Francoeur property has historical production of 163,657 ounces, which ceased in 1971 due to gold's fixed price of $35 per ounce, labor problems, rising costs and the federal government's removal of subsidies on gold production. The Francoeur is the company's most advanced project and, since a 50 percent operating interest was acquired in October of 1985, Rouyn has dewatered the shaft and rehabilitated the old workings to the 1,450-foot level. This year's program includes drifting, underground definition drilling to supplement the almost 50,000 feet of previous diamond drilling and the sinking of a second shaft. A surface drill program will test the extension of known gold zones and good potential exists for a substantial increase in reserves.

The results of the 1987 work program will contribute to

a feasibility study, which is expected early in 1988. Pending a positive feasibility study, production at a rate of 1,000 tons per day could be attained as early as late 1988. The company plans to construct its own milling facilities on its nearby Wasamac property but, in the interim, custom milling is available locally from several sources.

Also in 50 percent joint venture with Lac and located five miles east of the Lac Fortune and Francoeur projects, the Wasamac is a former producer with reserves of 946,185 tons averaging 0.149 ounces of gold per ton. In addition to this, a crown pillar containing 816,313 tons grading 0.099 ounces of gold per ton is scheduled to be mined via open-pit methods beginning in December 1987. Custom milling would begin in March 1988 and construction of a 750-ton-per-day mill will begin in the fall of 1987 and could be completed by late 1988. Plans to dewater the old Wasamac shaft and conduct an underground exploration are budgeted for $2.5 million.

Since June 1984, Rouyn management has raised $23 million, including an $11.1 million program to fund the 1987 program. Rouyn is well-financed and, due to the Lac association, no additional financing will be required. The involvement of Lac, coupled with its willingness to let Rouyn operate the jointly held projects, must be viewed by the markets as a vote of confidence. The high degree of probability associated with production at one or more of these projects is also likely to be reflected in the price of Rouyn shares.

(Rouyn Mining Resources Inc., 68 av. Principale, Rouyn-Noranda, PQ J9X 4P2, 819-797-2465.)

Startup Producers

Bull Run Gold Mines Ltd. (OTC:BULL)

Fully diluted: 9,250,000
Price: $4.25 (U.S.)

Bull Run is a U.S. company that holds a 40 percent working interest in the Big Springs gold project, jointly held with Freeport McMoRan Gold and slated for initial production in the fourth quarter of 1987. Located in Elko County, Nev., nine miles from Freeport's Jerritt Canyon mine, Bull Run probably seems to many investors to have been around forever.

BULL became widely known in 1982, when the price of its stock went from a low of $.19 to a high of $7.89 within 12 months. Since then, the stock has gone much lower, owing to the length of time required to evaluate a disseminated gold deposit, rare news from Freeport (the operator) and management's preference for a low market profile. The complex geology of the property and metallurgical problems also slowed the progress of the company, but with a production decision in February 1987, Bull Run is expected to attain gold production by year-end.

The ore at the Big Springs property is of two types: oxide, which will be treated by conventional heap-leach methods, and sulfide-type ores, which will require a roasting process to liberate the gold, followed by a conventional cyanide agitation process. The heap-leaching circuit will be operative by the end of 1987, with the roaster/cyanide circuit scheduled for completion by the third quarter of 1988. In full production, the mine is expected to produce 60,000 ounces of gold per year, with 24,000 of that accruing to Bull Run's account. Proven reserves in the North Sammy Creek and Mac Ridge ore bodies are estimated at 2.8 million tons with an average grade of 0.148 ounces of gold per ton; considerable exploration potential remains on the property.

The completion of a $13.5 million (U.S.) project financing (through Elders Resources Finance), imminent production, the potential for reserve expansion and the blue-chip association with Freeport are likely to result in significantly higher prices for Bull Run shareholders.

(Bull Run Gold Mines Ltd., 5290 Overpass Rd., Suite 225, Santa Barbara, CA 93111, 805-964-8894.)

International Platinum (T:IPN)

Fully diluted: 9,979,413
Price: $4.55

International Platinum is on the threshold of low-cost silver production at its Cobalt, Ont., property and IPN's portfolio of 21 platinum exploration properties is the most extensive in North America. Cash flow from oil and gas properties, coupled with recent private placements in the company and a reduced emphasis on flow-through financing should help the market in IPN shares.

Formerly Silver Lake Resources, International Platinum changed its name in 1986 to reflect its then-recent focus on platinum exploration. The company was formed in 1980 to explore and develop a silver property in northern Ontario. This property and several others ultimately deferred to the Silverside property, a high-grade vein deposit that the Cobalt area is known for and which is 50-50 joint ventured with Silverside Resources. The 150-ton-per-day gravity mill was scheduled for July 1987, with costs estimated at $4 per ounce.

Reserves are stated to be more than 3 million ounces, which would fund a highly profitable program over the three years of mine life outlined to date. Based on the history of this silver camp, the prospects for exploration potential are elsewhere on the property.

International Platinum entered the search for platinum before everyone else got on the bandwagon in 1986 and thus has assembled what many regard as the most impressive portfolio of platinum properties outside South Africa. Although most of them must be regarded as grassroots exploration, three stand out from the rest:

• Big Trout Lake—100 percent owned by IPN, this 9,600-acre property in northern Ontario has yielded excellent platinum and chromite values and a $750,000 diamond drilling will be completed in the 1987 field season.

• Fox River—This northern Manitoba property is within a 100-mile intrusion known as the Fox River Sill.

• IPN and partner BP Selco (earning a 60 percent interest for spending $1 million) have identified five platinum-bearing zones and geophysical surveys are under way to be followed by a diamond drilling program.

Recently, German metals giant Degussa agreed to fund $4.5 million of exploration on 15 of IPN's properties over the next three years. This association should add to the credibility of the search for platinum, as Degussa is seeking a North American source of concentrates for its Canadian and U.S. metals-refining operations.

In addition to the prospect of silver production and the

impressive array of platinum prospects, IPN has several gold properties that have yielded good results to date. The combination of all three metals, and especially the imminent production at Cobalt, makes IPN an unusually well-rounded junior stock.

(International Platinum Corp., P.O. Box 30, 150 King St. West, Toronto, ON M5H 1J9, 416-593-8706.)

Appendix II

Sources of Information

As might be imagined, I'm an advocate of spending money on information and advice related to investments, largely because I believe that one good idea will pay for years of investment advice. The challenge to investors is to figure out what advice is worth the price and, more important, what to do with advice once it's been bought and paid for.

General Publications

The Northern Miner—The *Miner* is *the* mining newspaper in North America, a publication that anyone interested in mining stocks should not be without. In addition to the best overview available on the North American mining scene—especially in Canada—the *Miner* publishes selective quotes from the Vancouver, Toronto, Montreal and Alberta stock exchanges. It also distills a weekly commentary on each market.

    The Northern Miner is essential for anyone who claims to have more than a one-shot, crap-shoot philosophy toward their penny mining investments. *The Northern Miner* also publishes the *Canadian Mines Handbook*, an annual anthology containing key facts on all Canadian mining companies, as well as the monthly *Northern Miner Magazine*. (*The Northern Miner*, $50/year (U.S.), 7 Labatt Ave., Toronto, ON M5A 3P2, 416-368-3481.)

Western Mining News—Published twice monthly, *WMN* features insider trading reports, notices of material changes in companies, Rule 144 sales, news announcements, Spokane quotes, and high/low prices and volume statistics on all Vancouver-listed companies. (*Western Mining News*, $55/year, N. 3019 Argonne Rd., Spokane, WA 99212, 509-922-4184.)

The National OTC Stock Journal—This weekly publication covers all types of penny stocks and, except for its monthly Vancouver market report, the primary emphasis is on U.S. companies not engaged in mining. Vancouver quotes are listed in the monthly Vancouver edition and only selectively in the weekly issues. (*The National OTC Stock Journal*, $89/year, 1780 S. Bellaire St., Denver, CO 80222, 303-758-9131.)

The Daily Bulletin—A daily summary of high, low and closing prices, volume statistics, names and stock symbols of all VSE-listed stocks. If you own a large number of stocks and follow them closely, this could be a handy adjunct to your research. Drawbacks include being at the mercy of the Canadian Postal Service and price, $475 for one year. Having a need to follow the market this closely almost presumes that you're working closely and actively with a broker; thus *The Daily Bulletin* may be superfluous for most of you—but still unexcelled for a definitive record. (*The Daily Bulletin*, $500/year (Canadian), Vancouver Stock

Exchange, P.O. Box 10333, 609 Granville St., Vancouver, BC V7Y 1H1, 604-689-3334.)

Vancouver Stockwatch—For the person who wants to follow developments in all Vancouver-listed companies and presumably takes an active approach to the market, *Stockwatch* is must reading. Editor John Woods writes a lively commentary on daily market activity, which precedes a section devoted to press releases issued by VSE-listed companies during that week.

Woods, a former floor trader turned broker/editor, recently introduced the selective use of charts and the regular listing of quotes with each press release. A *Toronto Stockwatch* debuted in mid-June 1987 and should prove as valuable to the TSE and Montreal investor as does the Vancouver version. (*Vancouver Stockwatch,* $395/year, P.O. Box 10371, Pacific Centre, 700 W. Georgia St., Vancouver, BC V7Y 1J6, 604-687-1500.)

VSE File—VSE File is a compilation of summaries of property reports and business plans, a listing of directors of VSE-listed companies and a stock option file arranged by company name, by individual and chronologically, with options expiring soonest listed first. Published quarterly, annual subscriptions are $350 (U.S. subscribers must remit in U.S. funds), and individual copies are available at $100 each. (Mining Software Services Ltd., 450 Shannon Way, Delta, BC V4M 2W5.)

Weekly Resource Stock Charts—Published monthly by Independent Survey Co., these charts of Canadian resource companies are essential to investors, even those who don't regard themselves as technical analysts. These charts go back two years and include price range and moving average data, volume charts, stock splits and capitalization figures. (Independent Survey Co., monthly, $232/year, single issues available for $23, P.O. Box 6000, Vancouver, BC, V6B 4B9 604-731-5777.)

Business News from Australia—Published by the Australian government, this is available free of charge from the Information Office at the Australian Embassy. It will help you follow developments in Australia. (Australian Embassy, 1601 Massachusetts Ave., N.W., Washington, DC 20036, 202-797-3000.)

Gold Stock News—Another publication that regularly addresses the Australian gold-share market. It also has affiliated brokerage services that can ably assist in the purchase of Australian gold equities. Another brokerage alternative is Barry Downs, a broker I've known for many years who now specializes in the Australian market. Barry is with Rotan Mosle in New York and can be reached at 212-750-0813. ($125/year, *Gold Stock News,* HMR Publishing, Box 471, Barrington, IL 60001.)

Australian Gold Shares—For those who want to know more about Australian gold shares, I recommend this recently updated book published by Australian brokerage firm Ord Minnett. ($95, Ord Minnett, 767 Third Ave., New York, NY 10017.)

Advisory Services

Penny Mining Stock Report—PMSR is my monthly newsletter, which is supplemented by a twice-monthly hotline on which I make buy and sell recommendations on specific stocks, update the progress of previous recommendations, discuss strategies and try to lend a sense of perspective to what's going on in the precious metals markets and in the penny mining stocks. I also conduct interviews with noted experts in the field of mining and investments and write about anything else that suits my fancy on the subject of mining. It goes without saying that I think it's required reading for anyone who owns, has owned or is thinking of owning a penny mining stock. (*Penny Mining Stock Report*, monthly, $139/year, P.O. Box 1217, Lafayette, CA 94549-1217, 415-283-4848).

The George Cross Newsletter—The daily *George Cross Newsletter* has been a fixture of the Vancouver market for the past 38 years. "George Cross" is the answer to the question, "Who knows more about more Vancouver stocks than anyone else on the street?"

Based on press releases from the companies and augmented by his years of experience and countless visits to properties, editor George Cross tries to make sense of what companies are saying and, in so doing, points investors toward companies he feels are worthy of attention. George's letter is not an advisory service in the normal sense of the word but instead requires readers to read between the lines. For the serious investor who wants to follow new stories as they develop, *The George Cross Newsletter* is both essential and money well spent. (*George Cross Newsletter, Ltd.*, daily, $300/year, P.O. Box 10363, Stock Exchange Tower, 609 Granville St., Vancouver, BC V7Y 1G5.)

Investing in Crisis—This is Doug Casey's monthly newsletter, and there's little question that Doug has introduced more investors to penny mining stocks than anyone else. In addition to frequent recommendations on mining stocks, Doug also addresses stocks, commodities and the economic Big Picture in the inimitable Casey style. (*Investing in Crisis*, monthly, $195/year, KCI Communications, Inc., 1101 King St., Suite 400, Alexandria, VA 22314, 800-832-2330.)

Canadian Penny Mines Analyst—This weekly newsletter and supplementary hotline are an offshoot of Marpep Publishing Ltd., which also publishes *Personal Wealth Reporter*. The *Canadian Penny Mines Analyst* is written by geologists for investors and does an excellent job of covering the Canadian mining scene. They keep readers abreast of previous recommendations, make several new recommendations with each issue and, unlike most other publications, also comment on stocks that should be avoided. (*Canadian Penny Mines Analyst*, weekly, $134/year, Marpep Publishing, Ltd., 133 Richmond St. West, Toronto, ON M5H 3M8, 416-869-1177).

Gold Stocks Advisory—*GSA* is an offshoot of Dan Rosenthal's excellent *Silver and Gold Report* and is a recent addition to the field of gold stock newsletters. Editor Jim Blakely conducts interviews with noted experts in the field, elicits their recommendations and follows up on them in subsequent issues. I serve on its board of editorial advisors. (*Gold Stocks Advisory*, monthly, $120/year, P.O. Box 20345, Columbus, OH 43220.)

Gold Stock News—*Gold Stock News* is a monthly newsletter that covers the North American and Australian mining scenes, with an emphasis on the high-capitalization mining companies. Edited by noted economists Alexander Paris and George Zagoudis, *GSN* also addresses the junior mining scene and covers Australia more completely than any other U.S.-based publication. (*Gold Stock News*, monthly, $125/year, P.O. Box 471, Barrington, IL 60011, 312-382-7857.)

The Jarl Aa. B. Whist Gold Letter—Editor Jarl Whist, president of Valhalla Energy, writes an in-depth commentary on the emerging Canadian gold producers and has a most enviable track record. At $300 per year, Whist is seeking an institutional audience, not your average newsletter subscriber. Subscribers who have been following his advice lately have been getting their money's worth. (*J.A.B.W.G.L.*, monthly, $300/year, $25 for sample copy, 814-837 W. Hastings St., Vancouver, BC V6C 1B6, 604-669-6656.)

...upTREND:—Henry Huber, a broker, covers the Vancouver market from a trader's perspective. He is a market technician who also relates the fundamentals in his monthly synopses of several companies. (*...upTREND:*, UPTREND Investment Services Ltd., monthly, $125/year, P.O. Box 49333, 4 Bentall Centre, Vancouver, BC V7X 1L4, 604-687-7990).

Sources for Quotes

"Bid & Ask"—This weekly carries summaries of quotations from the Vancouver, Montreal, Toronto and Alberta markets, as well as the Pacific and Spokane Stock Exchanges, key market indices and selected South African stocks. *"Bid & Ask"* is located in Vancouver, but they mail first class from Washington State. (*"Bid & Ask"*, $120/year, P.O. Box 3169, Blaine, WA 98230, 604-684-3186.)

InfoGlobe/MarketScan—Those of you who use computers to access investment information can get quotations daily through *Info Globe's MarketScan* data base. Info Globe also offers *The Northern Miner* online. I usually talk with several brokers and get selected quotes throughout the trading day, but this is the system I use to run my numbers at the end of each day (real-time quotes are *not* available on this system).

Fees vary by amount of usage. (InfoGlobe, 444 Front St. West, Toronto, ON M5V 2S9, 416-585-5250.)

Technical Publications

E&MJ (Engineering and Mining Journal)—Subscription rate outside the field of publication: $30/year, monthly. (P.O. Box 546, Highstown, NJ 08520-9990).

Heap and Dump Leaching, an International Newsletter—Just what it says it is. Subscriptions are $30/year in the U.S., U.S. possessions, Canada and Mexico, and $35/year in all other countries. Single issues are available for $5. (*DHL* Co., P.O. Box 26842, Lakewood, CO 80226-0842.)

Mine Development Bimonthly—$435/year (U.S.), airmail postage included. The "bible" of production costs, number of mine startups and other statistics on the mining industry. (*Mine Development Bimonthly*, Metals Economic Group, 1722 14th St., Boulder, CO 80302, 303-442-7501.)

Penny Mining Brokers

I know each of the brokers listed below and have done business with several of them. All are specialists in penny mining stocks and, in varying degrees, some are also quite active in nonresource venture-capital companies. Some are far more accessible than others: in several cases, you'll be dealing with assistant brokers, not the person listed.

Of the U.S. brokers listed, all offer IRAs and Keoghs. For the aggressive investor, owning penny mining stocks in these tax-deferred vehicles can represent an opportunity for rapid capital accumulation. Where no advice is sought, most

U.S. penny specialists are happy to execute orders for traditional stocks and usually offer substantial discounts on such trades.

In those instances where recommendations and advice are desired, the quality of the service is far more important than the rate of commission. In short, don't limit your search to Canadians just because you can save a few percentage points on commission. The quality of advice and skill of execution are far more important than what you pay for it. I can't vouch for everything the following brokers may want to do on your behalf, but I do know that they're all specialists in the field of penny mining shares—and that's the best place to begin looking for a broker who knows how to buy and trade these stocks.

United States

Darrell Brookstein, First Securities Northwest, Riviera Plaza, 1618 S.W. 1st, Portland, OR 97201, 800-547-4898.

John Brown, Eastern Capital Securities, Inc., 5 Century Dr., Suite 248, Greenville, SC 29607, 800-752-3233.

Ben A. Johnson, First Securities Northwest, Riviera Plaza, 1618 S.W. 1st, Suite 403, Portland, OR 97201, 800-547-4898.

Robert Nelson, Nelson Securities, N. 10 Post St., Suite 218, Spokane, WA 99201, 800-345-7593.

Jerry Pogue, National Securities Corp., 500 Union St., Suite 210, Seattle, WA 98101, 800-426-1608.

Dave Remark, National Securities Corp., 500 Union St., Suite 240, Seattle, WA 98101, 800-426-9494.

Michele Stell, Neidiger, Tucker, Bruner, Inc., 1675 Larimer, Suite 300, Denver, CO 80202, 800-525-3086.

Canada

Brock Aynsley, Midland Doherty, Ltd., 205 Bernard Ave., Kelowna, BC V1Y 6N2, 604-762-5577.

Robert Carrier, Osler, Wills, Bickle, Ltd., 1 Place Ville Marie, Suite 2101, Montreal, PQ H3B 4H5, 514-879-1770.

Gerry Fabbro, Midland Doherty, Ltd., Box 49020, 3 Bentall Centre, 11th Floor, 595 Burrard, Vancouver, BC V7X 1C3, 604-661-7764.

Frank Holmes, Merit Investment Corp., Suite 400, 155 University Ave., Toronto, ON M5H 2Z5, 416-867-6120.

Jim Love, McDermid St. Lawrence Ltd., Suite 1000, 601 W. Hastings St., Vancouver, BC V6B 5E2, 604-654-1110.

Ray Saadien, Canarim Investment Corp., P.O. Box 10337, Pacific Centre, 700 W. Georgia St., Vancouver, BC V7Y 1H2, 604-688-8151.

John Woods, Canarim Investment Corp., P.O. Box 10371, Pacific Centre, 700 W. Georgia St., Vancouver, BC V7X 1J6, 604-687-1500.

Stock Exchanges

Alberta Stock Exchange, 300 5th Ave. S.W., Third Floor, Suite 600, Calgary, AB T2P 3C4, 403-262-7791.

Montreal Stock Exchange, 800 Victoria Square, Suite 400, P.O. Box 61, Montreal, PQ H4Z 1A9, 514-871-2424.

Toronto Stock Exchange, Exchange Tower, 1 First Canadian Pl., Toronto, ON M5X 1J2, 416-947-4371.

Vancouver Stock Exchange, P.O. Box 10333, 609 Granville St., Suite 200, Vancouver, BC V7Y 1H1, 604-689-3334.

Winnipeg Stock Exchange, 167 Lombard Ave., Suite 955, Winnipeg, MB R3B 0V3, 204-942-8431.

Spokane Stock Exchange, 225 Peyton Bldg., Spokane, WA 99201, 509-624-4632.

The Stock Exchange Company Review Service, Exchange Centre, Bond St., P.O. Box H224, Sydney 2000, Australia.

Australian Associated Stock Exchanges, G.P.O. Box 520, Sydney 2001, Australia.

Securities Commissions

Superintendent of Brokers, Insurance & Real Estate (British Columbia Securities Commission), 865 Hornby St., Suite 1100, Vancouver, BC V6Z 2H4, 604-660-4800.

Registrar of Corporations & Securities, Government of Yukon, Dept. of Justice, Corporate Affairs Branch, P.O. Box 2703, Whitehorse, YT Y1A 2C6, 403-667-5623.

Alberta Securities Commission, 10025 Jasper Ave., Suite 2100, Edmonton, AB T5J 3B1, 403-427-5201.

Quebec Securities Commission, 800 Victoria Sq., Suite 1700, P.O. Box 246, Montreal, PQ H4Z 1G3, 514-873-5326.

Ontario Securities Commission, 20 Queens St. W., Suite 1800, P.O. Box 55, Toronto, ON M5H 3S8, 416-963-0211.

Securities & Exchange Commission, 450 5th St., N.W., Washington, DC 20549, 202-272-3100.

Appendix III

Bibliography

Bernstein, Jacob. *The Investor's Quotient.* New York: John Wiley and Sons, 1980.

Berton, Pierre. *The Klondike Fever—The Life and Death of the Last Great Gold Rush.* New York: Carrol and Graf, 1958.

Brown, Maurice P. *Mining Oil and Gas Explained.* Toronto: Northern Mining Press Ltd. 1981.

Casey, Douglas R. *Crisis Investing.* Atlanta: '76 Press, 1979.

British Columbia and Yukon Chamber of Mines, *Prospecting and Mining School.*

Girdwood, Charles P.; Jones, Lawrence F.; Lonn, George. *The Big Dome—Over Seventy Years of Mining in Canada.* Toronto: Cybergraphics Co. Inc., 1983.

Green, Timothy. *The New World of Gold.* New York: Walker and Co., 1981.

Hart, Matthew. *Golden Giant—Hemlo and the Rush for Canada's Gold.* Vancouver: Douglas and McIntyre, 1985.

Hart, Patricia and Nelson, Ivar. *Mining Town*. Seattle: University of Washington Press, 1984.

Hoffman, Arnold. *Free Gold*. New York: Rinehart and Co. Inc., 1947.

Ivosevic, Stanley W. *Gold and Silver Handbook*. Denver: Stanley W. Ivosevic, 1984.

Jastram, Roy W. *Silver—The Restless Metal*. New York: John Wiley and Sons, Inc., 1981.

Joralemon, Ira B. *The Unexpected in the Discovery of Ore Bodies*. New York: The American Institute of Mining and Metallurgical Engineers, 1930.

Keane, Frank. *The Vancouver Stock Exchange*. Vancouver: Chinook Communications, Inc., 1981.

Lamb, Norman. *Small Fortunes in Penny Gold Stocks*. Silver Spring, MD: The Penny Mining Prospector, 1982.

Lang, A.H. *Prospecting in Canada*. Ottawa: Canadian Government Publishing Center, 1970.

Lonn, George. *The Discoverers—A 50-Year History of the Prospector and Developers Association, Some Famous Prospectors and Their Discoveries*. Toronto: Pitt Publishing Ltd., 1982.

Mackay, Charles. *Extraordinary Popular Delusions and the Madness of Crowds*. New York: Harmony Books, 1980.

Mohide, Thomas Patrick. *Silver.* Ontario: Ministry of Natural Resources, 1985.

Neal, H.E. *Exploration and Mining Explained for Brokers and Market Watchers.* Toronto: Prospectors and Developers Association, 1985.

Rickard, T.A. *The Economics of Mining.* New York: Hill Publishing Co., 1907.

Rickard, T.A. *A History of American Mining.* New York: McGraw-Hill Book Co., Inc., 1932.

Rickard, T.A. *The Romance of Mining.* Toronto: The MacMillan Co. of Canada Ltd., 1945.

Ross, Alexander. *The Traders—Inside Canada's Stock Markets.* Toronto: Collins Publishers, 1984.

Smith, Duane A. *Colorado Mining—A Photographic History.* Alburquerque: University of New Mexico Press.

Stout, Koehler S. *The Profitable Small Mine—Prospecting to Production.* New York: McGraw-Hill, Inc., 1984.

Wells, Merle W. *Gold Camps and Silver Cities.* Moscow, Idaho: Idaho Department of Lands—Bureau of Mines and Geology, 1983.

Young, Otis E., Jr. *Western Mining.* Norman, Okla.: University of Oklahoma Press, 1970.

Appendix IV

Glossary

adit—A tunnel driven into the side of a hill or mountain through which a mineral deposit will be developed. An adit is often called a tunnel but, strictly, a tunnel is open at both ends. An adit is open only at one end.

alluvial, alluvium—Deposits of sedimentary material laid down in riverbeds, floodplains, lakes or at the foot of mountain slopes. Alluvial deposits are otherwise known as placer deposits.

alteration—Change in the mineralogical composition of a rock, typically brought about by the action of hydrothermal solutions.

anomaly—An abnormality in the earth's surface, detected by surveying and plotting geochemical or geophysical patterns over an area of ground. Anomalies suggest the possibility of mineral deposit, but only one in perhaps 1,000 or more leads to a mineral discovery that proves economical.

assay—The testing of a sample of mineralized rock to confirm the existence of valuable minerals, identify them individually and quantify their grade or purity.

assessment work—The amount of work specified by law that must be done each year to retain legal control of unpatented mining claims.

ball mill—A piece of milling equipment used to grind ore into small particles. Steel balls are used as the grinding medium, rotating with a large cylindrical drum.

base metals—Metals other than gold, silver, mercury and the platinum group. Copper, lead and zinc are base metals, so called because of their "inferior" status to precious metals.

bedrock—The solid rock of the earth's crust, usually covered by overburden of soil or water.

beneficiate—A term generally used to describe a preliminary mill treatment of iron ore that leaves the resulting product richer or more concentrated with minerals.

breccia—A type of rock whose components are angular in shape, as distinguished from a conglomerate whose components are water-worn into a rounded shape.

bulk sample—A large sample, frequently involving many tons, selected in such a manner as to be representative of the material being sampled.

claim—An area of land "claimed" by a prospector or mining company for the purpose of exploring a property, subject to certain restrictions. Claims are first staked out and then recorded in a government claim recording office. In Canada, a common claim size is 40 acres; in the United States, it is 20 acres.

concentrate—To treat ore so that the resulting "product" will contain less waste and more of the valuable mineral. Ore is often concentrated in a mill, then sent to a smelter whose end product goes to a refinery for the further elimination of impurities.

country rock—A loose term to describe the general mass of rock adjacent to an ore body, as distinguished from the vein or ore deposit itself.

core—A cylindrical piece of rock extracted from the earth by a diamond drill. A diamond bit at the end of the drill cuts the rock as it is driven into the earth. The cylindrical core is then removed to the surface for analysis of the mineral content and grade.

crosscut—A horizontal opening made underground from a vertical shaft or drift toward an ore body or vein and cut across the direction of the rock and the ore body.

depletion—The steadily declining amount of ore in a deposit that is being mined. Mines are said to be a "wasting asset" and minerals are often referred to as "depleting resources." Unlike oil, another depleting resource, most of the precious metals that have ever been mined are still in use.

development—All that is involved in bring a mining property to the production stage.

dilution—A lowering of the grade of ore being mined when waste rock (gangue) or low-grade ore is included in the mined ore. Dilution also refers to the reduced ownership position of shareholders when new shares of a company are issued.

dip—The angle at which a vein, structure or rock bed is inclined from the horizontal, measured at right angles to the strike.

disseminated ore—Ore carrying small particles of valuable minerals, spread more or less evenly throughout the host rock. Disseminated ore (low-grade) is distinct from massive ore (high-grade) wherein the valuable minerals occur in almost solid form with a much lower percentage of waste material.

dore—Gold and silver bullion that remains in a cupelling furnace after the lead has been oxidized and skimmed off.

drift—A horizontal passage underground. A drift follows the vein, as distinguished from a crosscut, which cuts across the vein.

drill—A machine for boring a circular core of rock that is recovered and examined for mineral content. A diamond drill powered by either compressed air, electricity, gas or diesel motor is very commonly used both on the surface and underground.

electrolytic—Pertaining to a refining process in which impure metal from a smelter is suspended in a cell containing a liquid known as electrolyte. The metal to be refined forms the positive post or "anode" and is deposited on the negative post, "cathode," by the electric current fed into the anode.

electromagnetic (EM)—The most important of the geophysical mineral-hunting techniques. Most EM equipment imposes or introduces electrical currents from above ground (on the surface or from the air) into the earth. This electrical activity is measured during and after the currents have passed through underlying rocks or mineral deposits.

fault—A break in the earth's crust caused by forces that have moved the rock from one side in relation to the other. Faults may extend for inches or miles and movement along a fault may vary widely. Ore deposits are commonly associated with faults, but not all faults contain ore bodies.

ferrous—Mineral that contains iron. "Non-ferrous" is a standard term for other minerals.

flotation—A common milling process in which certain minerals in solution attach themselves to bubbles and float to the surface, while others (less valuable or useless minerals) sink to the bottom, thus causing separation.

Fool's Gold—Popular name for iron pyrite, which is sometimes mistaken for gold and often found with it. Iron pyrite is hard and brittle, whereas gold is soft and malleable.

foot wall—The wall or rock on the lower side of a mineral deposit.

free milling—Ores of gold or silver from which gold or silver can be recovered by mechanical concentrating methods without resorting to roasting or chemical treatment.

gangue—The worthless minerals associated with valuable minerals in an ore deposit.

glory hole—An open cut or pit made in the earth's surface to reach and mine out an ore deposit near the surface. A glory hole also refers to a high-grade section of an ore body; extremely high-grade sections are sometimes known as "jewelry boxes."

gold nugget—A water-worn mass of placer gold (a form of natural gold) washed from the rock that contained it and deposited in riverbeds. Nuggets usually range in weight from approximately 30 grams to 50 kilograms. The heaviest nugget ever recorded, aptly named the "Welcome Stranger," was found in Australia in 1869 and weighed 90.9 kilograms, or 200 pounds.

grab sample—Rock samples usually taken from the best-looking material, which is then assayed to determine whether valuable elements are contained in the rock.

grade—Amount of valuable mineral in each ton of ore, usually expressed as a percentage for base metals and iron, in ounces or pounds for precious metals or uranium.

hanging wall—The wall or rock on the upper side of a vein or deposit.

high grade—Rich ore. As a verb, it refers to selective mining of the best ore in a deposit.

igneous rock—Rock formed by the solidification of molten material that originated within the earth.

leaching—A chemical process used in milling for the extraction of valuable minerals from ore. Also, the natural process by which ground water dissolves minerals.

lens—A body of ore that is thick in the middle, tapering toward each end.

level—A horizontal passage or tunnel in a mine from which ore is extracted. It is customary to mine an ore body from a shaft by establishing levels at regular intervals of depth.

lode—A mineral deposit in solid rock.

marginal ore deposits—Lower-grade ore bodies that are close to being uneconomical to mine. In a declining market for the commodity being mined, marginal ore deposits become subeconomic, as what was once ore once again becomes mineralized rock.

matte—Mineral in the course of recovery that comes from a smelter; it is not completely pure and requires refining.

metallurgy—The science and technology of metals. Process metallurgy is concerned with the extraction of metals from ores and with the refining of metals.

mill—The concentrate plant, usually at the mine site, that concentrates ore or treats ore so that the minerals are separated and prepared for ultimate recovery in pure form. A mill's output of concentrate will be in less bulky form than mined ore. (A "mill" in the strict sense is a machine used in the initial treatment process for grinding ore to the proper size for further treatment.)

mill heads—The average grade of ore fed into a mill.

muck—Ore or rock that has been broken by blasting. Miners who remove this ore are known as "muckers."

ore—Mineralized material in the ground that can be mined and processed for recovery of contained minerals at a profit. Ore is usually classified in one of three categories:

• *proven ore*—Also known as blocked-out, measured or positive ore. Developed by underground work or definitive drilling from the surface.

- *probable* or *indicated ore*—Outlined by diamond drilling and development on one side only, but not confirmed by full development work.

- *possible* or *inferred ore*—Inferred from geological projection and more general exploration drilling.

outcrop—Solid rock (bedrock) or mineral that is exposed on the earth's surface and can be examined visually.

overburden—Soil, plant life or water that covers bedrock.

pilot plant—Equipment set up on a small scale that will duplicate a practical production plant. The purpose of a pilot plant is to test methods of processing and recovering ore prior to making a commitment to build a full-scale plant.

placer—A sand and gravel deposit that contains small particles of a valuable mineral such as gold, platinum, tin or diamonds.

precambrian shield—The older rocks found in the Canadian Shield, a mineral-rich area covering almost half of Canada. Precambrian refers to that period of time ended 600 million years ago.

prospect—A potential mining property, the value of which has not been proven by exploration.

raise—A vertical or inclined underground tunnel that has been excavated upward from a lower level.

recovery—The amount of mineral in ore that is separated and recovered in a mill, usually expressed as a percentage per ton of ore treated.

refining—The final purification process of a metal or mineral (see *electrolytic*).

reserves—The measurement of the size of a mineral deposit, expressed as "proven," "probable" or "possible."

roasting—Treating ore, or a partly processed ore product, by a combination of heat and air to further remove impurities.

royalty—The amount paid by the lessee or operator to the owner of the mineral land, generally based on a certain amount per ton or a percentage of the total production or profits. Also, the fee paid for the right to use a patented process.

shaft—An opening cut downward from the surface for transporting personnel, equipment, supplies, ore and waste. It is also used for ventilation and as an auxiliary exit. It is often equipped with a surface hoist system that lowers and raises a cage in the shaft as well as "skips," or containers for bring up ore or waste.

smelting—The partial recovery of metal from process ore. The latter will have been treated and concentrated at the mill, but smelting is required to actually recover the metal content and convert it to a form that is ready for refining.

square set—A set of timbers used for support in underground mining.

staking—Measuring an area and marking it with stakes or posts to establish and acquire mineral rights.

station—An enlargement of a shaft or gallery on any level, used primarily for the storage and handling of equipment.

stope—A mining area established on an underground level where ore is blasted and broken.

strike—The direction, or the course of bearing, of a vein or rock formation measured on a horizontal surface.

strip—To remove overburden covering an ore body or underlying bedrock.

sump—An excavation for the purpose of catching or storing water. The bottom of a shaft is commonly used for this purpose.

tailings—Waste material from a mineral-processing mill.

vein—An open fissure or crack in rock containing mineralized material.

winze—A vertical or inclined internal shaft sunk from one level to another in a mine.

zone—An area or region that is distinct from the surrounding rock, either because of the type of structure of rocks or because of mineralization.

Index